Beyond the Dance Floor

Beyond the Dance Floor
Female DJs, Technology and Electronic Dance Music Culture

intellect Bristol, UK / Chicago, USA

First published in the UK in 2012 by
Intellect, The Mill, Parnall Road, Fishponds, Bristol, BS16 3JG, UK

First published in the USA in 2012 by
Intellect, The University of Chicago Press, 1427 E. 60th Street,
Chicago, IL 60637, USA

A catalogue record for this book is available from the
British Library.

Cover designer: Holly Rose
Copy-editor: MPS Technologies
Production manager: Tim Mitchell
Typesetting: Planman Technologies

ISBN 978-1-84150-566-4

Printed and bound by Hobbs, UK

To Nancy Gobatto and Dylan Rock (RIP), for
taking me to my first rave

Table of Contents

List of Figures

Acknowledgements

I want to begin by thanking the numerous women who were kind enough to donate their time to be interviewed for this study and answering so many follow up questions (for a list of names, see appendix). I hope that I have accurately captured their voices and spirits within the pages that follow. All of their words and actions inspired the completion of this project.

Many thanks to Tim Mitchell and the staff at Intellect Books for their patience, support and guidance in seeing this book through to its current form. I also owe a great deal to Diane Miller, whose editing expertise played an important role in shaping this project during the final hour.

I am also grateful for the mentoring and friendship of Kembew McLeod, who enthusiastically guided the completion of my dissertation, which served as the foundation for this project. Thom Swiss has been a great friend, mentor and co-author over the years, who deserves much thanks here, as do the remaining members of my dissertation committee while I was a graduation student in the Department of Communication at the University of Iowa: John Durham Peters, Kristine L. Munoz and Mark Andrejevic. Through their friendship and scholarship each of them has inspired this work in unique ways.

I would also like to acknowledge the departmental support I have received over the years from the School of Communication at Western Michigan University and the Department of Communication and Journalism at Oakland University, my current academic home. The patience and understanding of my Chair Jenn Heisler was vital to the completion of this project. Thank you also to the members of the US chapter of the International Association for the Study of Popular Music (IASPM-US) for their feedback and support over the years, as well as for giving my scholarship a home.

For providing careful and constructive feedback on various chapters of this manuscript, I thank Heather Addison, Kathleen Battles, and especially Kathryn Cady, Evelyn Ho and Vesta Silva for the time, energy and enthusiasm they dedicate to our year round writing group. Their friendship and support continues to be invaluable.

Interactions of all kinds with countless artists, friends and colleagues have also informed and inspired this work. I am especially appreciative for the support and insights of the following individuals along the way: Ashley Adams, Michael Mario Albrecht, Kim Alexander, Justin Burton, Matt Dunlop, Luis-Manuel Garcia, Carleton Gholz, Forest Green, Danielle

Wiese Leek, Amber Nixon, Tara Rodgers, Chris Smit, Zack Stiegler, Samira Vijghen and Ted Weinberg. My sincerest apologies to anyone whose name I have forgotten to include here. Thank you also to Michelle Habell-Pallan for inviting me to participate in the first Women Who Rock Conference in Seattle, Washington. It was an honour to dialogue about popular music in such a safe and inviting women-centred space. The strength and stories shared by members of the Ladies First hip hop collective at this conference were especially moving examples of the empowerment that is generated when music is used as a means of expression and collaboration.

Of course, in addition to the women interviewed here, I also want to acknowledge the courage and determination of all the ladies out there working within and beyond the boundaries of popular music, who embrace their challenges and pursue their passions in male-centric spaces of all sorts.

In particular, I would like to thank Nancy Gobatto for 30 years of friendship and for sharing with me her expertise in feminist theory. I will also forever be indebted to my brother, Konrad Farrugia, for his transcription services.

Finally, I am grateful to my husband Matt Dunstone for his unrelenting positivity about all things in life and to our son Leeland Dunstone for his daily reminders of the extraordinary pleasures that can be gleaned from life's seemingly mundane moments. And, of course, for their lifelong support my parents Anthony Farrugia, who took me to my first rock concert when I was 12, and Doreen Farrugia, for teaching me from a young age the importance of being an empowered woman.

Introduction

Coming of age in the 1990s, my knowledge of dance music was limited to what I heard on the radio and saw on television, and that music seemed antithetical to my New Wave and post-punk sensibilities. I occasionally heard the words 'house' and 'techno' and caught segments of *The New Dance Show* – a local, low-budget version of *Soul Train* – on Detroit television, yet I firmly believed that as a white, ethnic, Canadian girl, dance music had little to offer me. Too young to go to clubs and growing up before the advent of raves, I had no exposure during this time to underground dance music, despite living just across the river from Detroit. It would not be until the mid-1990s that I would rediscover the city through the sounds of techno.

Then, on a bone-chilling Saturday night one January when I was a university student, I encountered a style of dance music that was entirely different from what I had heard on the radio or at high school dances. It instantly satiated my musical appetite. As I reluctantly handed over ten dollars for admission to an elementary school on Windsor's west side, I had no sense of what I was about to experience.

Once inside, the space triggered memories of my own elementary school years, spent in a similar building across town. These recollections, which had been all but forgotten, along with the comforting warmth of the building were reason enough to pursue this adventure. So I ventured into a reconstructed space that was strobe-lit and lined with black plastic. With every step I took, the heavy bass beats emanating from the gymnasium became increasingly louder and more defined, aggressively luring me in.

As I entered the party space, two girls dancing face-to-face greeted me, their glow-in-the-dark nail polish shining brightly in the dimly lit space. Hundreds of people were present, dancing, their attention focused on the stage. The scene reminded me of an aerobics class, but one better suited to an alternate dimension, in which the uniform of choice included extra-wide pants and glow-in-the-dark accessories, and where participants experimented with innovative dance moves as the DJ relentlessly played a progression of other-worldly, electronic beats.

Throughout the course of the night, on a stage that normally hosts children's plays and band concerts, several DJs took turns contributing to the seamless and ceaseless electronic dance music (hereafter EDM) soundscape to which I danced for hours on end. As the midnight sky slowly turned to winter grey, the party finally came to an end. Hungry for more, on the way out the door I stuffed my pockets with flyers advertising upcoming events and a mixed tape handed to me by an aspiring DJ. Most of the parties I would attend over the next several years would take place in warehouses across the river in Detroit, a city best known for a different kind of music, a distinct sound that combined soul and pop to create the Motown Sound in the age of the civil rights movement.

So absorbed was I in learning the subcultural practices associated with EDM in my early raving days – familiarizing myself with DJ names and record labels, remembering to refer to songs as 'tracks', not to mention discovering where to shop for music and clothes while making new friends – that I took for granted the extent to which men dominated EDM culture. From the DJs and producers who performed Live PAs[1] to the club managers and promoters to the specialty record shop clerks, men held virtually every role of authority.

A year into these adventures I was fortunate enough to witness Detroit's own K-Hand (Kelli Hand) perform at a warehouse party. This was at a time when nothing more than a rope separated DJs from dancers, and I watched in awe as she dug through her record crates, pulling out and spinning track after track as the crowd howled and danced on. It was at this moment that I first began to wonder why I knew of no other female EDM DJs or producers, either in Detroit or elsewhere. In the years that followed I would see a handful of female artists perform, such as Minx and Punisher from Detroit or Montreal's Misstress Barbara, but overall women in EDM were few and far between.

In the late 1990s, EDM's popularity crossed over to the mainstream. Increased attendance at raves and club events produced a crowd of newcomers who were more conventional than their predecessors, creating a noticeable shift in the atmosphere. Traditional gender norms were adhered to more strictly, and men would often dominate the area in front of where the DJs performed. In some extreme circumstances their presence and actions were reminiscent of behaviour more typical of mosh pits at punk shows, where participants express their behaviour by pushing or slamming into one another. Women tended to congregate in bathrooms, where they touched up their make-up and socialized for hours on end. Although these EDM spaces purported to operate via their own subcultural rules and norms,[2] even on the most surface level traditional gender norms were still at play. Women were often distanced – physically, and at times even aurally – from the music and the technology so central to dance music and culture. For the most part they were relegated to the sidelines, encouraged to participate primarily as patrons on the dance floor.

Detroit's annual electronic music festival epitomizes the continuance of these normative practices. In 2000, Detroit hosted the first Detroit Electronic Music Festival. For months following the three-day festival, media sources commended organizers for the large turnout and the event's success in attracting people of diverse ages, races, genders and ethnicities. The *Detroit Free Press* claimed that the locally approved and sponsored festival drew the largest attendance of any annual festival in the city that year (McCollum 2001).

Since 2000 the festival has been an annual event that continues to develop and change. What was once a free experience now demands a significant enough financial investment that the merely curious no longer attend. The crowd tends to be less diverse than in its initial years, consisting mostly of white teens and young adults. Beginning with the endorsement of the Ford Motor Company, which used the festival as an opportunity to promote its newest vehicle, the Focus, in 2001, the festival has become increasingly commercial and now boasts sponsorship from companies such as Red Bull and Vitamin Water.

Unfortunately, one element that has changed little over the years is the lack of female DJs and producers invited to perform. Each year, women make up only a handful of the approximately 80–100 performing artists. The day after the 2001 festival I asked a local DJ-booking agent for her thoughts on the lack of female representation on the four main stages. None of her clients were women and she was aware of the festival's line-up of artists, but she still claimed that more women could be DJs and producers if they wanted to be.

Her response left me dissatisfied and disturbed enough to pursue the academic study of the complicated relationships at work regarding women's place in EDM culture. As I began to think more critically about women's roles in and their relationship to EDM, I sought to discern additional ways in which they are excluded from EDM culture, beyond the most physically obvious at events. Thus, the primary question this project seeks to answer is: What are the central historical, discursive, material and social practices that have impacted women's ability to secure powerful positions as DJs and producers in EDM culture? In documenting women's movement from bathrooms and dance floors to stages and studios, this project details the various practices that collectively have led to the marginalization of female DJs, as well as traces women's strategic and committed efforts to pursue their EDM interests in the 1990s and 2000s. Additionally, it contributes to and complicates the growing bodies of literature that lie at the intersections of popular culture, digital technologies and women's studies.

***

Theoretical Framings and Foundations

Scholars in the 2000s (Mazarella 2005; Kearney 2006; Driver 2007) began to pay increased attention to the proliferation of girls' media production. In her detailed exploration of this topic, Mary Celeste Kearney (2006) considers the impact and role of forces such as formal education, technological developments and the gendered identity ideologies that continue to be reproduced in everyday life. She spends the bulk of the conclusion to her book *Girls Make Media* lamenting the fact that in comparison to girls' progress in engaging video and computer technologies, their contributions to popular music have increased little over the years.

Looking back on the 1990s, the time in which she began her research on girls' media production, Kearney notes that 'the number of female youth interested in expressing themselves through writing songs, playing instruments, and recording music dropped off considerably over the course of the [decade]' (294). She cites several reasons for this, including the expense of music production and the reality that music has traditionally been a performative medium that leaves behind few material products.

I agree with Kearney that girls have had less success participating or having their voices heard in popular music; even today relatively few women produce EDM at a professional level despite the availability of affordable computer technology. Yet since the 1990s and especially into the 2000s, girls and women have made some inroads into popular music spaces beyond the consumptive practices of fans. For instance, their participation has grown considerably in the area of DJing, which involves mixing together previously recorded tracks. Nevertheless, the socially constructed, patriarchal culture that Kearney argues infuses girls' day-to-day experiences and accounts for their relatively minimal impact in popular music remains an issue for women not only in EDM but across popular music genres (Cohen 1997; Whiteley 1998; Leonard 2006; Reddington 2007). Although the number of women exploring DJing and producing is growing exponentially, they continue to be minority players in the EDM culture worldwide.

Using EDM as a case study, this book addresses the ways in which certain historical, discursive, social and material practices in EDM replicate hegemonic ideas about gender, technology and power, while other practices work to destabilize and intervene in these discourses. To varying degrees, each chapter is concerned with analysing discursive practices of some kind, including those related to EDM texts, notions of community, technology, feminism and feminist practices, as well as music industry and studio politics. I use the phrase 'discursive practices' to refer to various elements of analysis, including the verbal articulations of the women whose voices appear here. Additionally, I also use the term in a Foucauldian sense (1980) to refer to the conditions that produce social, historical and political knowledge systems, which are imbued with power and that in turn constitute people's everyday lived, material reality.

Since the 1990s the number of women who have moved from the dance floor to secure a place behind the decks has steadily increased. From time to time, popular dance music magazines such as *XLR8R*, *Urb* and *Mixer* have featured female DJs and producers. On occasion, women have even graced the covers of these glossy, high profile print magazines. Moreover, some of the women who have broken through DJ culture's glass ceiling –including some of the participants in this study – are reluctant to see gender as an issue in EDM and DJ culture.

Despite the claims of some women that gender is a non-issue in EDM, I believe that contextualizing this project in a feminist framework is essential to understanding the gendered power dynamics that govern these spaces. In other words, even though many of the women interviewed did not personally identify as feminists or with feminism, their discourses and actions reflect feminist concerns and objectives.

Thus, the primary interest that shapes this study are the various strategies that women employ to try to break through the discourses, ethics and practices-what Foucault (1988) refers to as the 'technologies of the self'-that normalize DJing and producing as male undertakings. To this effect, the project explores how women individually and collectively work to acquire not only specific skills, but also certain attitudes that augment their agency. In other words, I am interested in how women negotiate being agentic selves in the male-dominated EDM environments in which they participate.

Given these concerns, it is important to clarify what this project is and what it is not. Rooted in an interdisciplinary cultural studies framework, this book is concerned with how women negotiate their place within the existing relations of power in EDM and DJ culture. As such, although it is a critical study of women's experiences in a popular music genre, it is not a study in popular or critical musicology. Whereas popular musicology's primary concern is with criticism and analysis of the music itself, popular music studies primarily tend to focus on social and cultural context (Scott 2009).[3] However, this is not to deny that there are overlapping points of interest between this book's focus and musicological concerns. Similar to Sheila Whiteley's (2000) work addressing the music industry's sexist attitudes and Susan McClary's focus on subjectivity (2004) and underrated female musicians such as early blues singers Bessie Smith and Ma Rainey (2000), this project analyses EDM's sexism and brings to light the efforts of female EDM artists to overcome it.

Understanding the practices and experiences of female EDM artists requires examining the range of historical, discursive and material practices that have shaped and continue to shape EDM and DJ culture. Similar to other cultural studies projects, this book is concerned with the ways in which people struggle over reality and their place in it, where they are 'continuously working with and within already existing relations of power, to make sense of and improve their lives' (Grossberg 1998: 201). For the purposes of this project I use the term 'culture' broadly to signify 'the production of meaning, or "signifying practice" that happens at every level of the social and at every moment within cultural processes' (Gray 2002: 12). Consequently, I take an interdisciplinary approach to the study of women in EDM by employing a range of theoretical and methodological approaches drawn from media studies, popular music studies, cultural studies, women's studies, technology studies and cyber studies. Collectively, these fields inform the central objectives guiding this study.

Aims and objectives

I was initially drawn to this project by an interest in why male EDM DJs continue to significantly outnumber females despite girls' and women's inroads into media and cultural practices such as film-making and web design. At this time in the early 2000s women were also experiencing increased access to music and technology due to the advent of personal computers, the Internet and digital music files such as mp3s. From here my interest expanded to a consideration of the gendered power dynamics of EDM and DJ culture and how they have been maintained over time. Thus, the primary objective of this book is to uncover and understand the intricate and nuanced ways in which a host of practices – historical, discursive, material and social – have contributed to the male-centricity of EDM culture and thus the marginalization of women in these spaces. A second aim of this project is to discover the personal struggles and successes of female EDM artists as well as the collective strategies they employ to carve out spaces for themselves in EDM and DJ culture.

As a result, this study also serves the archival purpose of documenting women's musical and technological experiences and efforts at a particular historical moment. Along these same lines, my findings constitute a case study that details contemporary women's understandings of, perspectives on and relationship to feminism.

Moreover, the processes of women's artistic and technological efforts at a grass-roots level are rarely explored. By presenting the voices of female DJs and producers, this project validates their experiences and publicizes both their artistic musical practices and their resourceful efforts to build supportive, women-centred EDM spaces. The documentation of such labour is significant because it is through everyday practices that gender norms are defined and reproduced, and hence gendered power dynamics sustained both within and beyond popular music scenes and genres. Additionally, while there are revisionist histories, ethnographic and critical accounts of women in hip hop, punk and indie rock, this book is one of the first to focus on female EDM artists specifically. Thus, it makes an important scholarly contribution to several academic disciplines but most importantly to the field of popular music studies where research on women and EDM is still in its infancy.

Gender and sound

Even though a close examination of EDM's design principles – its beats and rhythms – is not a primary objective of this study, it is important to briefly examine the relationship between gender and sound in EDM before turning to an explanation of the methods this study employs. Understanding the relationship between gender and sound in EDM is important because it addresses the presence of gendered assumptions about musical taste in EDM culture but also explains why sound is not a focal point of this study.

At times, discussions of EDM's physical properties evoke gendered associations. EDM's defining characteristics are its predominant reliance on electronic instruments and tools and its very limited inclusion of lyrical content. As an electronically based musical form, by definition it invokes associations with masculinity and men, as technology continues to be discursively and materially framed in masculine terms. As Chapters 1 and 5 will argue, these associations are among the reasons why so few women produce EDM. However, they do not seem to account for the sonic stylistic choices those few female producers make. It is noteworthy that while some DJs and producers perceive differences between men's and women's EDM inclinations, my findings suggest that for the most part genre preferences, DJ mixing approaches and production styles cannot be delineated along gender lines.

The gendering of music and discourses about music have a long history. In her influential text *Feminist Endings*, McClary (1991) argues for more critical analysis and understanding of how gender identity is encoded musically. In one example, she calls attention to gendered metaphors in music theory commonly used to classify cadence types or endings. These metaphors are rooted in the *Harvard Dictionary of Music*, which includes the following entry:

> A cadence or ending is called 'masculine' if the final chord of a phrase or section occurs on the strong beat and 'feminine' if it is postponed to fall on a weak beat. The masculine ending must be considered the normal one, while the feminine ending is preferred in more romantic styles.
>
> (cited in McClary 1991: 9)

McClary (1991) goes on to explain that the elements of the binary opposition masculine/feminine are differentiated on the basis of relative strength, with 'masculine' representing a strong beat and 'feminine' a weak beat. In this manner, the association of strong beats with masculinity partially accounts for the gendering of rock as male.

Sara Cohen (1997) argues that rock is produced as male through the labelling of its physical properties and by the everyday activities that comprise the rock music scene. I want to begin by focusing on Cohen's first claim, which is a discursive move fuelled by the work of music critics. As I discuss further in Chapter 1, critics – who are overwhelmingly male – favour traits typically associated with men and masculinity, such as rawness, aggressive intensity and violence. In contrast, they reserve feminine descriptors such as 'soft' and 'light' for negative reviews (McLeod 2002). Critics' persistent use of such terms to describe music reinforces an association between good music and men, and between bad music and women. Further, it reinscribes the popular belief that men are more knowledgeable about and have better taste in music than women. Ramifications of these assumptions and beliefs are present in EDM culture.

To illustrate this point, I turn to a post from a thread titled 'Women and Electronic Music' that appeared on the 313 listserv, a mailing list dedicated to the discussion of a particular subgenre of EDM, Detroit techno.

> I am one of the girls that frequently gets pushed out of the way while trainspotting and [watching] the way DJs are moving their hands or twisting knobs. Many guys I just meet snub me out of conversations for a while till I spit some knowledge ... I love when some guy looks through my crate and is like, 'Ummm, whoa, u have nice records [and] *u actually have some techno.*'
>
> (5 October 2000, emphasis added)

This woman's experiences speak directly to the ways in which women are often shut out of EDM conversations because men presume they are ignorant about EDM and have little to contribute. What is even more telling about this post is the writer's observation that men are surprised and impressed that she has techno records. The assumption within EDM culture is that techno's futuristic science-fiction themes and hard, industrial sounds do not appeal to women.

To be fair, some women also believe that men and women prefer different styles. In an interview featured in *The Advocate*, the Los Angeles-based tribal progressive DJ Kimberly S. states that 'for the women I play a diverse set – anything from hip-hop and R&B to very vocally flavored house music, disco, and funk'. By comparison, 'for the boys I start light, then go for a progressive tribal sound, flavored with vocal anthems, with a lot of crescendos and climaxes to keep the energy high' (Barrett 2001: 77). Based on her DJ experiences, Kimberly S. believes that men respond more positively to DJ sets that build up to a driving, aggressive, high-energy sound whereas women prefer dancing to music that is less intense and more melodic and lyrical.

My intention here is not to dismiss the experiences of Kimberly S. or other DJs who agree with or share her experiences, but rather to highlight a significant finding of this project that is antithetical to these views. The EDM artists that I interviewed DJ and produce an eclectic and extensive range of music. The genres the DJs described as having in their collections include breakbeat, breaks, drum 'n' bass, jungle, dubstep, electro, ghetto tech, glam, hip hop, house, acid house, hard house, house, deep house, progressive house, tech-house, IDM (intelligent dance music), techno, micro techno, minimal techno, progressive, psychedelic-trance, trance and tribal; and even this extensive and far-reaching list is by no means definitive. The work of the producers interviewed for this study is equally diverse.

Furthermore, Tara Rodger's (2010) interviews with a range of female electronic music artists suggests that while female musicians may approach the studio environment differently from one another, there is no clear indication that their gender influences their practices. These points are noteworthy because they speak to how these women's musical tastes and practices do not correspond to societal expectations or assumptions about the relationship between gender and the consumption and production of EDM.

Through their tastes and practices, women are challenging assumptions and reshaping beliefs about where women's interests in EDM lie. In Chapter 2 I argue that EDM culture is not as faceless as it once was as DJs and celebrities are increasingly one and the same. Nevertheless, the absence of lyrics in most EDM genres and subgenres prevents women from falling readily into typical, gendered traps in which their contributions are viewed only in terms of vocals and/or lyrics, regardless of the actual range of their contributions. The divergent tastes, interests and skills of women DJs and producers suggest their potential to move EDM in new directions.

Methodology

This research employs ethnographic methods and textual analysis to explore the relationships between EDM producers, texts, the industry and, indirectly audiences. The examination of popular EDM discourses is vital to understanding how women have been and continue to be valued, discussed and positioned in EDM and DJ culture. Thus, in addition to drawing on scholarly work, my analyses also utilize a range of EDM texts, artefacts and spaces including magazines (such as *Urb, XLR8R* and *Mixer*), websites (including *Shejay* and Sister SF), discussion lists (Sisterdjs) and an extensive personal collection of EDM that includes tracks and DJ sets produced by the women interviewed for this project.

With reference to textual analysis, Angela McRobbie (1994) argues that 'looking not only at the finished products, the visual and verbal texts, but also at the professional ideologies alerts us to wider social changes, to social connections across otherwise conceptually separate spheres' (165). In other words, textual analysis is most effective when it moves beyond the text itself and considers the relationship between an artefact and its context. For this reason I have drawn on both textual analysis and ethnographic methods in researching and writing this book.

To capture the experiences of women in EDM and the context of EDM culture, I conducted interviews; engaged in participant observation; 'hung around' (Willis 1991) record stores and DJ practice spaces, including bedrooms and studios; and attended events in a range of locations including parks, deserts, warehouses and clubs. This project is a 'theoretically informed' ethnographic study in that it presupposes shifts back and forth between induction and deduction (Willis and Trondman 2002: 396, 399). Such shifts emphasize the importance of everyday cultural practices as understood from below while also viewing them within a particular historical context. Following Willis and Trondman (2002), in articulating how these lived social relations embody, mediate and enact the operations and results of unequal power, I do not assume an ethnographic authority that positions the researcher outside of the field of study. Rather, I am aware of my own positionality in the world and the ways in which it has shaped and informed this narrative of women and EDM.

Accordingly, in addition to textual sources, the book draws on dozens of formal and informal personal interviews with women involved in EDM culture. The semi-structured, formal face-to-face interviews I conducted with 35 women who self-identified as EDM DJs and/or producers and two MCs[4] structure the chapters that follow. Most of the interviews took place in the San Francisco Bay Area from 2003 to 2005, with follow-up interviews completed via phone and email. Several women were interviewed more than once, which added depth to the project as it allowed me to trace changes and developments in their participation in EDM culture. Interviews and supplementary ethnographic fieldwork were conducted between 2003 and 2008 in Portland, Oregon; Los Angeles, California; San Diego, California; Iowa City, Iowa; Detroit, Michigan; and Chicago, Illinois. Follow-up interviews with many participants continued online and by telephone through 2010.

Despite initially developing an interest in this subject matter in Detroit, I chose the San Francisco Bay Area as my principal research site because of the significant number of female DJs in this geographical region. At the time of my fieldwork, it was also the home of Sister SF, the longest-running female DJ collective in the United States (1997–2007). Chapter 4 presents a case study of the collective and its expansion to include chapters in New York City; Portland, Oregon; and Denver, Colorado.

In her discussion on women in indie rock, Marion Leonard (2006) argues that case material on individual musicians is valuable because it 'reveals shifting relationships and balances of power between artists and industry bodies as the career of a band develops' (13). The personal interviews in this study highlight the viewpoints of female DJs and producers, which are omitted from most print and web-based writing on EDM culture. In particular, the women interviewed divulged information related to identity construction and community building, and discussed their experiences dealing with various levels of the industry and with such personnel as record label owners, club management and event promoters. To help ensure the accuracy of direct quotes, face-to-face interviews were recorded onto mini-disc and later transcribed, while phone interviews involved note-taking in real time. Additional information was collected via email.

The women interviewed ranged from amateurs to professionals, with most falling somewhere in between. That is, they had experience performing in public and were often paid for their work, but they did not consider themselves full time DJs/producers. While a few of the interviewees were reluctant to give their age, the remainder of those who participated were between 18 and 40 years old at the time of the interviews. Similar to Leonard's (2006) experiences with women in indie rock, almost all of the women were white, with the exception of two Asian Americans and two African Americans. Although most of the early producers of EDM in the United States in the late 1980s were young Latino and African American men, EDM culture was quickly appropriated by white America, in large part due to the popularity of rave culture and its appeal to white, middle-class youth. Thus, the racial composition of the participants in this study reflects the high proportion of white participants in EDM culture overall.

Participant observation

As my opening narrative illustrates, I have been a fan of EDM and a participant in the EDM networks since the mid-1990s, when I first immersed myself in rave culture and began attending EDM events in the United States, Canada and on a few occasions Western Europe. I also began participating in the Internet-based discussion boards related to EDM, attending net-meets, collecting music that spanned a range of EDM subgenres and amassing EDM-related magazines, event flyers and newspaper articles. For a brief time I collected vinyl records and experimented with DJing firsthand after purchasing a set of Technics 1200 turntables in the early 2000s. The 'insider' knowledge I had as a result of my extensive participation in EDM culture played a large part in how this project took shape. Most importantly, many of the women I interviewed expressed considerable surprise upon meeting me to find that we had so much in common. I defied their stereotypes of what an academic researcher was supposed to be, in that I was also a young woman in my 20s who shared their passion for EDM.

Researchers studying the goth scene (Hodkinson 2002), indie rock (Leonard 2006) and punks (Reddington 2007) have also commented on the benefits of 'insider status' for researchers. My familiarity with EDM proved especially important in discussions about music and music scenes, because EDM is continuously fracturing into more and more subgenres (McLeod 2001). Without prior knowledge of EDM subgenre sounds and scenes and the terminology used to describe them, one could easily get lost in these conversations. Accordingly, interviews usually took the form of open-ended, semi-structured conversations, after which I was often given mix CDs created by the interviewees or invited to share a meal or attend an event at which they were performing. Yet because my personal DJ experiences were short-lived and confined to my bedroom walls and because I have not attempted – at least not with any seriousness – to produce EDM, I am not a 'true insider' for the purposes of this project.

In pursuing this research, I have also considered the impact that reflecting on my questions has had on the women who so graciously donated their time and shared their insights and experiences. Some participants seemed to have previously thought a great deal about the issues raised in our conversations, while for others our meetings presented an opportunity for them to consider for the first time the issues – including the gendering of technology, the representation of female DJs and the process of identity negotiation – that have impacted their efforts to carve out spaces for themselves in these male-dominated environments. In the pages that follow I do my best to present the women's experiences as they conveyed them, providing a key to analysing the gendered power relations that structure and govern women's place in EDM culture.

Outline of chapters

My examination of women and EDM culture is organized into six chapters. Chapter 1 articulates the connections between the historical and contemporary discursive and material dimensions of the relationships between gender, technology and popular music. It begins with a discussion of the changing relationship between women and technology over the course of the twentieth century, focusing specifically on how the masculinization of technology has impacted women's relationship to music technologies. From here I turn to the development of EDM and DJ culture and the impact of the 1990s Riot Grrrl culture. In essence, this chapter is concerned with the myriad historical, social and material factors that have created an unequal distribution of power in EDM culture, and with the impact of these relations on women specifically.

The first chapter to draw on interview material, Chapter 2, focuses on the ways in which the physicality of female artists is implicated in their EDM efforts in a culture that privileges hyper-feminine, hetero-normative representations of women. More specifically, it considers how these artists personally and publicly negotiate their identities in an increasingly commercialized environment that often privileges image over skill and in which the distinction between celebrity and DJ is increasingly blurred. Analysing mediated representations of women DJs, the chapter articulates the ways in which the experiences of interviewees have been circumscribed by the narrow range of identities offered to women DJs by EDM texts and popular culture more generally.

Chapter 3 examines the influence of geographical and Internet-based networks on women's ability to communicate with one another, locally and globally, about their EDM experiences on personal and professional levels. These unique spaces provide women with networking opportunities that in turn increase their subcultural and social capital with respect to EDM. The three distinct environments highlighted in this chapter include monthly potluck meetings in Portland, Oregon; the Sisterdjs listerv; and *Shejay*, a comprehensive e-zine and website dedicated to the discussion of women in EDM.

Using Sister SF – the longest running women-centred DJ collective in the United States – as the subject of a case study, Chapter 4 interweaves and expands upon several of the themes discussed in earlier chapters. Specifically, it examines the collective's perspective, strategies and struggles over the course of its ten-year history. The complicated dynamics at play within the group and in its rhetoric include the decision not to identify as feminist, despite what appear to be feminist practices. These dynamics also include the negotiation of practices that embody a do-it-yourself, grass-roots approach on the one hand, and those that more closely typify commercial/corporate practices on the other.

Moving beyond DJs, Chapter 5 addresses the impact of the gender–technology connection discussed in Chapter 1 on women's cultural production – and lack thereof – as EDM producers. It considers the ways in which the politics and gendered division of labour typically found in the music industry and recording studios have limited women's access to the material (e.g. technology) and discursive (e.g. technical language) practices needed to acquire necessary knowledge and skills. Highlighting examples of successful female EDM producers, it also brings to light some of the strategies women have adopted, including formal education and collaboration, to not only produce EDM but also connect with distribution outlets.

The conclusion presents an overview of the study's findings and suggests potential avenues for future scholarship, in an effort to move the claims and findings discussed throughout the book beyond the EDM context. A section of Chapter 3 draws on material previously published in *Women's Studies in Communication*. Earlier versions of Chapters 4 and 5 have been published in *Feminist Media Studies* and *Current Musicology*, respectively.

Notes

1. The term 'Live PA' stands for Live Performance Artist. It is used in this context to refer to a live EDM performance as opposed to the playing of pre-recorded music packaged in various formats, including record, CD or MP3.

2. EDM and rave culture at the time promoted a philosophy of peace, love, unity and respect (PLUR) built on a shared sense of community (Silcott 1999).
3. For a detailed study of EDM's musicological structure, see Mark J. Butler (2006): *Unlocking the Groove: Rhythm, Meter, and Musical Design in Electronic Dance Music*. Bloomington, IN: Indiana University Press.
4. Generally, the role of the MC (Master of Ceremonies) in EDM culture is to rhyme or sing on top of music played by the DJ, often for the purpose of 'hyping up' the crowd.

Chapter 1

Critical Connections: Gender, Technology and Popular
Music Cultures

In her book *Bedroom DJ: A Beginner's Guide* (2003), Piper Terrett takes readers on a journey from her beginnings as an amateur DJ's heartbroken ex-girlfriend, to wondering if women could be DJs, to finally becoming a DJ herself. Her audience is privy to the frustrations and doubts she experiences over the course of her DJ education. Early on she describes the 'horrifying' task of putting together a set of turntables she has purchased. In this moment of exasperation, she reasons that 'maybe this was why guys were DJs and birds were told to stick to hobbies like knitting and trying to lose weight. After all, us girls knew it was blokes that like the fiddling with bits of metal' (18). In her frustration, Terrett expresses the widespread belief that technology is the business of men – a belief she goes on to defy by becoming a DJ herself.

The purpose of this chapter is to contextualize how this modern-day relationship between gender and technology – one in which it is normal for women to knit but not to fiddle with metal – first emerged and subsequently became naturalized. The chapter explores how the normalization of this relationship affects women's access to music technologies and the spaces and networks in which they circulate. To understand these articulations, this chapter traces the historical, discursive and material practices that have shaped technology and music cultures along gender lines.

I first articulate some broad historical connections between gender and technology before moving on to explore the specific gendered relationships that have developed in relation to audio and music technologies. Next, the male-centricity of music subcultures and women's response to their subordinate status in these spaces is examined. Specifically, a review of the early 1990s Riot Grrrl movement will reveal some of the strategies young women adopted to create spaces for their voices in punk rock music's male-dominated culture in the United States and Britain. To contextualize the experiences of the female EDM DJs and producers featured in subsequent chapters, the remainder of this chapter centres on the origins of and gender dynamics at play in EDM and DJ culture.

The gender-technology connection

In her foreword to *Machina Ex Dea: Feminist Perspectives on Technology*, Ruth Hubbard (1983) argued, 'there is no denying that women tend to be users of machines and men their inventors, makers, and repairers' (vii). Cynthia Cockburn (1985) echoed this sentiment a few years later when she stated that women 'may push the buttons but they may not meddle with the works' (12). Twenty years after Hubbard and Cockburn's commentary on women's relationships to technology, sociologist Judy Wajcman (2004) continued to argue that despite the expansion of women's independence stemming from paid labour and widespread public discourse about gender equity, the connection between masculinity and technology remains strong.

Feminist and cultural studies scholars alike agree that technology is not inherently masculine, but has been labeled as such as a result of socially constructed narratives, rhetorical devices and material practices. Over the course of the twentieth century such influences have narrowed the definition of what constitutes technology and systematically written women out of technology's collective memory. Previously, in the nineteenth century, the term 'technology' was readily applied to the skills of bakers, farmers and teachers, as well as engineers. In this context the knitters Terrett refers to would indeed have been considered technologists; however, in her contemporary context they serve as a counterpoint to technology tinkerers.

Beginning in the early twentieth century, a plethora of autobiographies were published that revitalized a middle-class identity for men and specifically linked their expertise and knowledge in science and engineering to technology, which in turn redefined the term (Oldenziel 1999). In Oldenziel's words, 'in the course of a century, technology had been turned into a product, engineers into producers, and women and workers into consumers who were mere onlookers of the technical enterprise' (50). Oldenziel goes on to discuss the ways in which these discursive practices worked specifically to position engineers as the new technological heroes.

Since the 1980s, numerous scholars (Wajcman 1991; Cockburn and Ormrod 1993; Ormrod 1995; Green 2001; Wajcman 2004) have argued that the meanings of both gender and technology are discursively and socially constructed through everyday practices, whereby 'technology is best understood as a social as well as technical process which blends seamlessly with the everyday' (Green 2001: 175). The power that technology affords 'produces knowledges, meanings and values, and permits certain practices as opposed to others' (Ormrod 1995: 35). The social construction of the relationship between gender and technology has created an atmosphere in which 'femininity is incompatible with technological competence; to feel technically competent is to feel manly' (Cockburn 1985: 12). Thus, the situating of women as always already outside invention and technology naturalizes and preserves a seemingly innate relationship between men and technology.

The framing of technological interests as not only natural but also defining features of masculinity is widespread in popular culture, beginning in early childhood. At the time of this writing a search for the phrases 'toys for boys' and 'toys for girls' on Amazon.com produced the following results: the top ten recommended toys for boys included a monster truck custom shop, tool kit, science kit and rocket kit. For girls, a jewellery box, tea set, cookware and bracelet-making kit were included in the top ten. These 'girl toys' foster the development of skills that today fall outside of the purview of technology.

A hopeful note may be found in the one item that appears on the top ten lists for both boys and girls: a Multi Voice Changer by Toysmith. Though it looks like a simple megaphone, its purpose is reminiscent of some electronic musician production gear; it features ten different voice modifiers that can create hundreds of voice combinations. This example notwithstanding, for the most part toys that speak to modern-day technologies are marketed to boys much more than to girls.

Audio technologies and gender

As a result of the historical, discursive and material practices that frame technology – including music and audio technologies – as men's interests, women's positionality and mobility across popular music genres and within the popular music industry have been restricted. This book contributes to the ongoing discussion of how and why popular music industries, scenes and practices continue to be male-centric spaces. Overwhelmingly, men occupy the powerful positions in these environments, dominating the lists of DJs, rock stars, critics, sound engineers and even avid collectors. The male-centricity of popular music can be traced back to early music technologies such as the phonograph and radio, which were themselves packaged, advertised and sold along gender lines (Carlat 1998; Kenney 1999).

When it was first mass-marketed to the public in the 1920s, radio's place in the home was uncertain, but it did not take long for manufacturers to perceive and reinforce gender differences concerning its use. From the earliest days when amateurs tinkered with wireless sets and used radio technology to explore aurally distant cities, such practices were considered to be the hobbies of boys and men, despite evidence of some female amateur operators (Anon 1916). In contrast, following the invention of broadcasting, radio came to be viewed predominantly as a technology to acculturate the family, which was regarded as women's work (Carlat 1998). However, compared to men women were already viewed as being more passive users, who desired simple radio sets. Consequently, manufacturers began to make easy-to-use, female-friendly models, but curiously, they were still advertised almost exclusively to men. Carlat attributes this seeming contradiction to advertisers' belief that women might be interested in radios as furniture or a source of entertainment, but men would be the ones to instigate and carry out the purchasing of radio receivers. Thus, for most of the 1920s radio ads in *The New York Times* for example ran in the Sunday sections that also featured automobiles and airplanes, two other predominantly male concerns. Another strategy the editors of the trade publication *Radio Merchandizing* suggested was for radio dealers to place female mannequins 'reclining in languorous positions' in store-front displays to attract male customers (editors of *Radio Merchandizing* 'The Female of the Species is More Attractive Than the Male', as cited in Carlat 127).

In addition to being labeled as passive users, women also experienced marginalization in the radio industry as executives and on-air announcers. Despite considerable success in these roles in the industry's early years, they were squeezed out in the 1930s as the pay and prestige associated with such positions increased (Douglas 1987). This occurred despite the success of announcers like Halloween Martin, whose popular early morning wake-up programme 'The Musical Clock' featured her playing phonograph records, making Martin one of the nation's first real disc jockeys. For the most part women's involvement in the production of radio was primarily relegated to turning out vacuum tubes by the thousands on mass-production lines. Thus, despite some exceptions, women occupied few powerful roles in radio as the industry's success increased; instead, they were viewed as passive consumers, whose control was limited to turning a dial.

In the 1960s, the advent of high fidelity (hi-fi) technology and its discursive construction in popular culture continued to solidify the seemingly natural relationship between audio and music technologies and men. It was not just hi-fi sound that was marketed to men, but more importantly, complex hi-fi technology, which came in separate components as opposed to the simpler, more integrated equipment geared towards women (Taylor 2001: 80). Advertisements in trade magazines such as *HiFi & Music Review* and mainstream publications like *Newsweek* portrayed hi-fi technology as a means for men to escape from domestic concerns and family life. In contrast to television, which was depicted as a passive, feminine technology, 'men used hi-fi sound reproduction technology (including its necessary adjunct, the Long Play (LP) record album) to produce a domestic space gendered as masculine' (Keightley 1996: 150). Further contributing to the masculinization of hi-fi technology, it was also common for such articles and advertisements to suggest that women considered the excessive volume of hi-fi systems oppressive (Keightley 1996). Specifically, the circulation of these discursive and material practices worked to distance women from cultivating an interest in using these technologies, which over time imprinted a cultural discourse of women's technical ineptitude that further dissociated them from these 'masculine' technologies.

This distancing contributed to limiting women's participation in music scenes to less powerful, more passive roles compared to those available to men. Keeping within traditional notions of femininity, women in music are still generally expected to participate in music scenes in ways that are already coded as 'feminine' (Green 1997: 28), for example, as dancers or singers as opposed to electric guitarists, drummers or DJs. Music education scholar Lucy Green (1997) observes that media coverage tends to focus on lead singers, and because more women sing than play instruments, these depictions affirm 'the correctness of the fact of what is absent: the unsuitability of any serious and lasting connection between woman and instrument, woman and technology' (29).

Similarly, Barbara Bradby (1993) comments that in dance music women are usually included in disturbingly traditional representations – as dancers and vocalists – and are not only objectified but often remain anonymous. They receive little or no credit for their contributions and are rarely the topic of conversation in the specialist dance music press, in comparison to the male music producers, who become known as the creative minds behind these feminine displays. This ideological divide between images of women as performers and men as producers devalues women's role in music making and casts doubt on female creativity in general (Lisa Lewis 1990, cited in Keyes 2002: 208).

Further preventing women from interacting with audio and music technologies is the association between femininity and classroom-approved music – such as classical – compared to popular music, which generally is not taught in the classroom and is considered masculine. This is important because in Green's (2005) words, 'musical experience itself, in the context of the school, actually produces and reproduces not only gendered musical practices but gender identities and with them, gender itself' (89). As a result, like the contexts discussed above, the classroom is another space in which gendered relations to audio and music technologies continue to be systematically reproduced. The following section details the ways in which music-based subcultures that transpire 'on the streets' or in other male spaces have historically marginalized girls and women and limited their agency and power. The Riot Grrrl movement is included as an example of an intervention in the male-dominated punk rock music subculture.

Women and music subcultures

The term 'subculture' has historically been used to refer to groups of young people and their positioning in opposition to the dominant culture or parent group (Thornton 1997). It also generally implies some degree of deviant behaviour. I do not consider women in EDM to constitute a subculture, not only because of the variation in their ages, politics and interests, but also because I do not believe they can be categorized as a single collective group with an interest in differentiating themselves from dominant society. Additionally, scholars (Stahl 2004; Muggleton and Weinzierl 2004) have begun to question the existence of subcultures in our global, Internet age. Nonetheless, an understanding of women's historical place in music subcultures is useful here for two reasons. First, it provides the context for examining the positionality of women in EDM culture; and second, it foregrounds issues of power, agency, identity and community that are central to this discussion.

Scholars at the Birmingham Centre for Cultural Studies were some of the first to study subcultures, most of which were rooted in music (Hall and Jefferson 1976). In response to these early studies (Hall and Whannel 1965; Arnold 1973; Clarke 2007), Angela McRobbie and Jennifer Garber (1975/1997) expressed concern over the Center's lack of interest in how girls negotiate leisure space. They argued that when girls appear in scholarly work on subcultures 'it is either in ways which uncritically reinforce the stereotypical image of women with which we are now so familiar … or else they are fleetingly and marginally presented' (112). To be fair to the scholars they critique, McRobbie and Garber outline some of the practical reasons for this depiction of girls in subcultural studies in the United Kingdom at the time. For instance, girls' wages were lower than those of boys, which left them with less money to spend on subcultural activities or accessories such as music. Also, popular magazines perpetuated ideas of femininity that relegated girls' culture to the bedroom, at least until the emergence of mod culture in the 1960s whose embrace of fashion provided an opportunity for the recognition of girls' interests in style in public subcultural spaces. Young women were also directed to focus on the home and marriage as opposed to 'hanging out in the streets' and participating in 'authentic' subcultural activities that were predicated on challenging dominant culture. However, McRobbie and Garbner argue that in only studying activities that had an 'elsewhere' – that took place beyond the private space of the home – and were rooted in oppositional ideologies and practices, the Birmingham Centre's early research legitimated the notion that only such activities were authentic and research worthy. In effect, because girls' activities did not display the same kind of opposition, they were deemed insignificant and inauthentic. In turn, researchers ignored them despite the pleasure, participation and power they afforded girls.

Notions of resistance and delinquency were also at the core of many early subcultural studies that focused on male youths (Hall and Jefferson 1976; Hebdige 1979; Brake 1985). Scholars viewed their participation in subcultural activities as defiant acts that challenged dominant culture and presumably the capitalist system by which it is governed. In turn, these music subcultures, such as punk in the 1970s, were viewed as heavily rooted in rebellion.

More recent studies have shown that girls and women, though fewer in number, have always been present in historically masculine subcultures like punk rock and continue to participate in increasing numbers. Unfortunately, their participation is often overlooked. In her ethnographic study of punk girls, Lauraine Leblanc (1999) argues that 'these girls' lives, experiences, and opinions have remained unarticulated within the subculture, and invisible to the public' (64). Punk itself was primarily cultural and heavily rooted in fashion, and thus dependent on the knowledge and skills of girls (McRobbie 1994: 145). Nevertheless, girls were cast in the role of sideline participants early on as punk became associated with a rebellious ideology, unruly behaviour, hanging out in the streets of London and New York, and an investment in fast, hard music.

In contrast to the punk rock ethos of male rebellion, girls' involvement in music has long been associated with consumerism and viewed as complacent with dominant cultural values. Girls' musical interests were thus seen as antithetical to subcultural and hence creative practices. The interests of young women have been presented as uncreative and inherently passive, despite McRobbie's (1994) argument that consumption is part of all youth cultures and has the potential to be a transformative process with the power to subvert mainstream culture. She uses the London rag market in the 1990s – which consists of shops and stalls that sell secondhand or vintage-style clothing – as an example of a site of entrepreneurial activity that offers young people the opportunity to destabilize the system by selling and buying high fashion cheaply. McRobbie notes that 'the more modest practices of buying and selling have remained women's work and have been of little interest to those concerned with youth cultural resistance' (1994: 137).

In many cases, the efforts of women who chose to play instruments and form bands have been either overlooked or written out of the picture by both popular media and scholars across locations, times and genres. Writing on women in punk bands, Helen Reddington (2003) presents an alternative history of punk that places women instrumentalists at the foreground of the British punk movement in the 1970s. Yet, Reddington argues, journalists and sociologists have completely ignored these women and their contributions.

Similarly, in her revisionist history of early hip hop culture, Guevara (1996) foregrounds the 'distinct and essential creative role of *women* in the formation and development of hip-hop' in the 1980s (47, italics in original). She publicizes the ways in which key elements of hip hop culture, such as rapping, breakdancing and graffiti writing, developed exclusively as competition between males. In the case of graffiti writing, women such as the legendary Lady Pink and Lady Heart acknowledge the support they have received from male graffiti masters; yet Guevara notes that 'the competition that typically exists among writers takes on a special character when applied to women, as in the constant charge of "biting" (copying someone else's style) brought against female writers by any number of males' (52). In response to these exclusionary practices, many girls and women have since taken a do-it-yourself (DIY) approach to creating girl- or women-centred spaces in male-dominated music cultures.

Riot Grrrls, representation and subcultural infrastructures

Feeling marginalized in the punk subculture in the 1990s, young women in the United States and Britain formed bands grounded in a punk DIY ethic that challenged popular ideas of femininity and girlhood and undermined the notion that punk rock music was an exclusively male domain. Bands like Bikini Kill and Bratmobile in the United States and Huggy Bear in the United Kingdom drew attention to image and body-related issues by writing the words 'slut' and 'bitch' on their limbs and midriffs to neutralize sexist terms. Their music was hard and their lyrics addressed girls' and women's issues such as eating disorders, the beauty myth, date rape and oral sex. They promoted their messages in handouts such as the one Bikini Kill and Huggy Bear passed out on their joint tour, which read 'I really wanna look at female faces while I perform. I want HER to know that she is included in this show, that what we are doing is for her to CRITICIZE/LAUGH AT/BE INSPIRED BY/HATE/WHATEVER' (Leonard 1997: 234). Riot Grrrl bands provided a liberatory space for young women at their concerts by encouraging them to take physical control over the space of the concert and in their everyday lives by questioning their objectification and limited power in society.

As the 1990s wore on women were more easily able to distribute their music and convey messages via the women-run Internet distribution companies that sold their products (Piano 2004; Kearney 2006). As Piano (2004) points out,

[I]t is in 'doing' (making zines, playing in bands, reading zines, organizing conferences) rather than in 'being' (viewed as a spectacle) that participants become group members, and consequently, where the potential for political intervention and group affiliation can take place.

(254)

In other words, women in rock have begun to successfully bypass gatekeeping structures to engage in the production of music. Through the formation of all-female bands and record labels and girl-centred zines, young women are developing their own infrastructures and creating spaces for girls and women in punk culture. The movement is also opening up dialogue about the possibilities for girls and women in other male-dominated music cultures.

The well-documented history of the Riot Grrrl movement is particularly important to the study of women in EDM, because it offers an earlier example of women who successfully challenged the male-centricity of the punk rock music genre and the punk subculture. Additionally, even though women in EDM do not share a common political stance or interest in subverting hegemonic representations of womanhood, their efforts and public actions as DJs and producers themselves challenge traditional representations of girls and women in music-based cultures – sub-, post-, or otherwise. To outline EDM's gatekeeping processes and their impact on female DJs and producers, I next present a brief overview of the history and positioning of women in EDM and DJ culture.

The roots of EDM DJ practices

A predominant characteristic that distinguishes EDM DJs from other types of DJs is the conception of the DJ's set as one seamless, continuous mix without breaks between tracks. This practice was first conceptualized in the late 1960s. Influenced by new music that included fast soul songs, funk by James Brown and lasciviously rhythmic Latin tracks (Poschardt 1998 105), DJs sought to provide a constant flow of music to keep people dancing throughout the night. The technological innovations of the 1970s, coupled with this innovative DJ technique, enabled disco to fully emerge as a musical and cultural form distinct from its predecessors.

In 1975 record companies introduced the 12-inch single, which replaced the shorter 7-inch single. The new format offered better sound quality and made it easier for DJs to pinpoint specific locations in the tracks. Around this time there were also developments in hardware, including specially designed turntables and mixers to suit this new style of DJing (Reynolds 1999: 271). The technology enabled beat matching – the practice of playing two different records in time with one another – and further facilitated the ascent of the DJ-auteur. DJs went from being viewed as programmers to being regarded as fully fledged musical artists as they seamlessly layered and mixed in and out of different musical tracks. Reynolds (1999) describes this ability to create unique musical sets as 'one that's closer to improvising on a musical instrument, or playing with a plastic, mutable substance' (271).

In the 1980s, parties that featured DJs and dance music turned into garage sessions and illegal raves (Poschardt 1998: 105). In 1987, after a summer of dancing all night in clubs in Ibiza Spain, London DJ and club promoter Paul Oakenfold returned to England with 'a complete subcultural package of slang, behavior, and clothing' (Reynolds 1999: 58). Because of laws that restricted club operating hours, people wanting to dance all night in England began turning to illegal warehouse parties. Fueled by the 'love drug' ecstasy, these events marked the beginning of a new music-based culture that became a global phenomenon in the 1990s.

Concurrently, innovative EDM sounds were being created across the United States. From the remnants of disco, house music emerged in Chicago in 1986, and over the next few years it heavily influenced the development of techno in Detroit and garage in New York City. By the early 1990s the popularity of EDM and rave culture in the United States had expanded beyond the Midwest and East Coast to locales such as Dallas, Texas in the Southwest and Los Angeles and San Francisco along the West Coast (Sicko 1999). While EDM continued to grow and subdivide throughout the remainder of the 1990s, little attention was paid to the activities and contributions of women on either side of the Atlantic, regardless of their growing presence in major urban areas such as San Francisco.

Women's efforts were dismissed not only within EDM culture but also in both popular and scholarly writings on EDM. A case in point is Dan Sicko's (1999) history of the evolution of techno music in Detroit. Similar to other accounts of EDM subgenres such as house and trance (Fikentscher 2000; Taylor 2001), and DJ and rave culture (Poschardt 1998; Reynolds 1999; Silcott 1999), Sicko's *Techno Rebels: The Renegades of Electronic Funk* centres on the creative production of men, in his case the musical output of young African American men in the late 1980s and 1990s in the Motor City.

While it is true that men have constituted the majority of the active participants in EDM culture, women have also contributed to its global growth and development. However, similar to what happened to women in punk rock (Reddington 2007) and hip hop (Rose 1994), women's efforts in EDM have often gone undocumented. In his otherwise comprehensive narrative, for example, Sicko does not so much as mention the names of native Detroit EDM artists such as Kelli Hand and DJ Minx, despite the worldwide recognition they have garnered for their production and DJ efforts.

The gender divide in EDM and DJ culture

Commenting on women's place in DJ culture, Brewster and Broughton (2000) note that throughout history DJs have overwhelmingly been male. They preface their use of the pronoun 'he' throughout their book on the history of the DJ by noting, 'Throughout this book the DJ is "he" and this is not just a matter of grammatical simplicity. In DJing's 94 years, women have been largely frozen out of the picture, with precious few exceptions' (377). They go on to claim that fresh EDM scenes introduce new possibilities for women to become DJs, but end their discussion of gender here. Although few women have received notoriety as DJs until quite recently, the ongoing reference to the DJ as 'he' works discursively to maintain maleness as essential to pursuing DJing and in turn precludes even the intimation that women can be DJs. Using Sicko's book published in 1999 – well after Kellie Hand and Minx were active in the local Detroit EDM scene – as a case in point, it continues to be 'his-story' that is privileged in writings on DJ culture.

Given the extent to which technology in general and music technologies in particular have been carefully constructed as male since the beginning of the twentieth century (Théberge 1991; Keightley 1996; Oldenziel 1999), it is not surprising that EDM has developed as a male-centric space that mirrors most other popular music genres and the mainstream music industry. Moreover, it is true that most of EDM's pioneers were men, who relied heavily on digital audio technologies including drum machines, samplers and turntables to make their music. Noting the gender divisions within the dance music industry in the 1990s, McRobbie (1994) observed that EDM reproduced 'the same sexual division of labour which exist[ed] not just in the pop music industry but in most other types of work and employment' (170).

For the most part, over the course of the 1990s women continued to take part in EDM culture as dance floor participants as opposed to organizers or performers (McRobbie 1994; Redhead et al. 1998; Reynolds 1999; Silcott 1999). When they did engage in roles beyond the dance floor, they were usually in low-level positions such as helping out on the till, working behind the bar or distributing flyers on the streets and in clubs (McRobbie 1994). This is not to dismiss women's participation in these capacities, but rather to highlight how women's ability to pursue both power and pleasure further up the hierarchy of rave and DJ culture was limited.

Writing in the early 1990s, Barbara Bradby noted that moving into DJing and/or producing was an arduous process for women because they were 'equated with sexuality, the body, emotion and nature in dance music, while men have been assigned to the realm of culture, technology, language' (Bradby 1993: 157). Even in the abundant research related to sampling and digital music technologies written since Bradby's claim (Théberge 1997; Taylor 2001; Frith 2003; McLeod 2005), the fact that men constitute the majority of these musical artists is seldom a point of discussion.[1] Accordingly, the changing climate of sexual politics discussed in third wave feminist discourse and popularized in popular music circles via the Riot Grrrl movement in the 1990s has not been noticeably reflected in EDM culture. This point is addressed in much more detail in the chapters that follow.

The homosociality of record collecting is another central factor that has historically contributed to the male-centrity of EDM culture. In *Club Cultures*, Sarah Thornton (1996) builds on the work of Pierre Bourdieu to address the social logic of club/rave culture and its relationship to the mass media. She draws attention to the masculine bias of 'subcultural capital' (11) – that is the rules that govern a particular subculture – and describes the processes by which it is objectified and embodied. Assessing the leisure practices of young men and women, Thornton claims that the first choice for an evening out for women between the ages of 15 and 24 in Britain is a dance club, but that the primary reason they go to clubs is to dance after having spent most of their money on clothes and cosmetics, and not necessarily to learn about the latest record releases. Men, on the other hand, invest a greater amount of capital in record purchases and are more likely to spend their time at clubs networking with DJs and music producers, which builds their subcultural capital. Chapter 3 examines in depth the networking strategies female DJs have adopted to increase their social and subcultural EDM capital.

However, music consumption patterns were not always stratified along gender lines. From 1890 to 1930, when records were first introduced for domestic consumption, women were regarded as the primary audience for recorded music (Kenney 1999). In the nineteenth century, playing the piano was one of the ways women were expected to contribute to the refinement of the private sphere of the home. Since recorded music was introduced at the height of the piano's popularity, music consumption was coded as feminine, with most men believing themselves too masculine to ever become musicians. Thus, when they were first introduced to the masses, records were primarily marketed and sold to women, who played them mainly during the day while their husbands were at work and their children at school. Even most record store clerks at the time were women, so that 'phonograph shopping often amounted to a total women's social experience' (Kenney 1999: 96). Yet the latter half of the twentieth century saw a complete reversal of that norm. That the act of record collecting experienced such a thorough gender shift over the course of a century speaks to the extent to which such practices are socially constructed via the discursive and material practices of a given time period.

The significance of record collecting

The value and utility of collecting lies in the function of record collections as 'carriers of the information whose arrangement and interpretation is part of the broader discourse about popular music' (Straw 1997: 5). In this sense such collections display Foucault's understanding that knowledge is power; because men have typically invested most heavily in collecting music, collecting itself becomes part of the gatekeeping process that can dissuade women from becoming DJs. In response to the gains made by Grrrls (3 r's) and other women in rock, Will Straw (1997) comments that 'having learned to play guitars and play them loud, women find that the lines of exclusion are now elsewhere. They emerge when the music is over, and the boys in the band go back to discussing their record collections' (15).

The significance of collecting is even more pronounced in DJ culture, where one's performance is heavily dependent on her music collection. It is an even more substantial issue in EDM DJ culture because of the limited opportunities available to learn about EDM, even in the Internet age. The sophistication of EDM, which is broken down into genres and innumerable sub-subgenres (McLeod 2001), along with the countless number of record labels and artists, renders knowledge of the music – which changes rapidly – difficult to acquire and maintain. Despite the availability of the music online, successful searching requires a knowledge of insider terminology and other strategies for sifting through the clutter.

The organization of EDM in specialty record shops by subgenres and labels was more likely to mystify naïve consumers than to offer an inviting learning space, especially for women. As EDM grew in popularity in the 1990s, these male-dominated spaces became central hubs where knowledge was shared and social networks developed between collectors, producers and DJs. Emphasizing the significance of these spaces in the 1990s, Dave Haslam (1998) went so far as to assert that 'the mutually beneficial relationship of record shop and specialist DJ [was] integral in keeping scenes alive' (152). Regrettably, in keeping these scenes alive these spaces also maintained record collecting as a homosocial interest and a source of camaraderie exclusive to men.

Writing on the techno subgenre specifically, Simon Reynolds (1999) attests that,

> the presence of women on the dance floor is not reflected by the proportion of women in the ranks of professional DJs … This has a lot to do with the homosocial nature of techno: tricks of the trade are passed down from mentors to male acolytes. DJ-ing and sample-based music also go hand in hand with an obsessive 'trainspotter' mentality: the amassing of huge collections of records, the accumulation of exhaustive and arcane information about labels, producers, and auteurs.
>
> (274)

During the height of vinyl's popularity in the 1990s, 'white labels' were popular status symbols among DJs. These 12-inch vinyl singles contained no details about their producers or labels. Thus, even in the physical presence of the DJ, these tracks could remain unknown and serve as yet another gatekeeping device. Additionally, in the United States dance music received virtually no airtime on broadcast radio or music video channels or in mainstream music magazines such as *Rolling Stone* or *Spin*. Thus, one had to be connected to DJs, producers and others 'in the know' to access the important details of which Reynolds speaks. Because these individuals were mostly men it remained difficult for women to acquire this essential knowledge. The proliferation of such information on the Internet since this time has increased women's access to such information.

DJ rebels

The importance given to esoteric knowledge in DJ culture has a great deal to do with the role of the DJ in club and rave culture. The DJ is expected to go above and beyond simply playing music to communicate with the dance floor. Drawing on his personal experience as an EDM DJ, writes that, a key skill is obviously not just to drop the popular, well-known songs at the right part of the night, but to pick the right new releases, track down the obscurer tunes and newest imports, get hold of next month's big tune this month; you gather this pile, this tinder, together, then you work the records, mix them, drop them, cut them, scratch them, melt them, beat them all together until they unite.

(151)

In other words, the DJ is no longer expected simply to play music as record companies have released it. The assessment of a DJ's skills often depends on his or her ability to successfully scavenge, then seamlessly mix in and out of, records. In other words, 'The DJ constructs the raw material of sundry tracks into a metatrack, an abstract emotional narrative with peaks and valleys' (Reynolds 1999: 273). Hence, good DJ sets are sometimes referred to as 'journeys' and good DJs regarded as artists who have achieved priestly proportions (Haslam 1997).

Characterizing the role of the DJ further, Reynolds (1999) goes so far as to describe DJing as an activity that 'depends on a certain arrogance, a propensity for characterizing oneself as an authority, a leader ... DJs often style themselves as crusaders fighting for a cause' (275). This view of DJing as a heroic and/or rebellious act is reflected in the titles of the books *Last Night a DJ Saved My Life* (Brewster and Broughton 2000) and *Techno Rebels* (Sicko 1999). Similarly, on event flyers DJs are literally described as 'masculine, musical superheroes, powerful conquerors who control and dominate the crowd' (Herman 2006: 28–29). In contrast, even when female DJs appear on public relations (PR) materials they are rarely rhetorically constructed along the same lines, despite early rave culture's philosophical grounding in PLUR – peace, love, unity and respect. These gender inequalities speak to Simon Reynolds' (1998) assessment that even at rave's height, PLUR was more myth than reality.

Social and gender relations in rave culture

In the 1990s, when raves were the primary venues for EDM, EDM culture and rave culture were synonymous in many respects. Typically, raves were held in warehouses or other spaces that were often completely transformed into utopian theme parties, with elaborate light and sound systems designed to completely shut out the outside world. Scholars took notice of this new subculture and began to comment on its impact, meaning and potential to transform everyday social relations for participants. In an overwhelmingly positive review of rave culture, Daniel Martin (1999) claimed that 'the hierarchies in rave culture are less damaging to those at the bottom than the hierarchies found in other subcultures and in the dominant social order' (87).

In terms of the dance floor, Martin's point is well taken. For instance, the stylistic androgyny of rave participants in the United States, whose distinct fashions favoured baggy clothes and baseball caps, subverted women's classic position on the dance floor as objects of the male gaze. Maria Pini's (2001) research on female rave participants supports this notion. Pini writes:

> For many women, rave represents an undoing of the traditional cultural associations between dancing, drugged 'dressed-up' women and sexual invitation, and as such opens up a new space for the exploration of new forms of identity and pleasure.
>
> (154)

In interviews with female ravers in the United Kingdom, Pini (2001) found additional instances of gender role transgression for women on the dance floor.

> [This] is a group which tends *not* to be thought of in terms of 'expertise', and which presents very different questions when it comes to issues of sexual and personal safety, domestic responsibility and culturally specific notions about 'appropriate' sexed being.
>
> (67)

Women spoke freely to Pini about their participation in drug culture or their comfort in going by themselves to all-night events, experiences that are often off limits to women. Gilbert and Pearson (1999) have suggested that the dance floor is also potentially liberating for men because the art of dance has historically been marginalized and deemed feminine in western society.

Returning to Martin's claim, it is important to note that the equality he speaks of does not apply to participation further up the ladder for DJs or producers. His only subsequent reference to hierarchies appears implicitly in his elaboration that EDM 'decenters the subject, refusing the pop star or the cultural icon as the glorified subject' (92–93). Others agree that unlike most popular music genres, dance music audiences place greater emphasis on genre than on performer identities (Hesmondhalgh 1998). However, as I elaborate in Chapter 2, this mindset has shifted considerably since the 1990s.

As the 1990s drew to a close, so did rave culture's popularity in the United States. For some participants raves became too mainstream, while others simply outgrew the subculture (Anderson 2009). Additionally, the increased pressure and crackdowns from law enforcement dramatically reduced the number of illegal events promoters were willing to organize. At this point, EDM moved from rave spaces to more legitimate club venues.

Since 2000, in this post-PLUR environment, the DJ's status has become much more significant as the DJ's celebrity is touted to attract customers to clubs. This way of thinking differs greatly from that of the rave space, in which despite the reverence for DJs *all* participants were thought to be important to shaping the dynamics of an event. In the post-rave climate, the sense of freedom the women in Pini's study experienced on the dance floor is difficult to acquire on the stage. The implications of the rise of the celebrity DJ for female DJs are discussed at length in Chapter 2.

Conclusion

This chapter has traced the historical, discursive and material practices related to technology, gender and subcultural music practices that have constructed women's place in EDM and DJ culture. The chapter began by examining how the narrow redefinition of technology in the early twentieth century limited the term's application to male-dominated science and technology fields. The articulation of technology as masculine contributed to the masculinization of music technologies and cultures over the course of the twentieth century, as marketing efforts focused on selling complex audio technology components to men.

The marginalization of women with respect to technological interests and practices extends to music subcultures and music production, where women's efforts have been routinely overlooked. The homosociality of elements of DJ culture such as record collecting and references to DJs as dominating conquerors further marginalizes women in these spaces, positioning them as outsiders and preventing them from acquiring EDM information and skills. Thus, the freedom women experience on the dance floor is not reflected on the stage or in production studios. The following chapter considers the range of identities available to women DJs and explores how, in a post-feminist cultural context that views DJs as commodities, women have publicly negotiated these identities.

Note

1. One exception is T. Rodgers (2003) 'On the Process and Aesthetics of Sampling in Electronic Music Production', *Organized Sound*, 8: 3, pp. 313–320. Although gender issues are not directly addressed in this discussion of the musical and political dimensions of sampling, Rodgers does include interviews with female electronic musicians including Kathleen Hanna, formerly of the Riot Grrrl band Bikini Kill.

Chapter 2

Sex Kittens, T-Shirt DJs and Dykes: Negotiating Identities in an Era of DJ Commodification

B y and large, raves and clubs have been the venues in which most people are exposed to and consume EDM in the United States. EDM rarely receives the radio play given to other genres such as hip hop, which is the country's electronic music of choice. In contrast to hip hop, which originated in the late 1970s in the inner-city African American and Latino communities of New York's South Bronx, EDM has no clear-cut origin story. As I describe in Chapter 1, its emergence cannot be pinpointed to one specific geographic location in the United States or elsewhere, and it has never had direct ties to a particular race or class.

For critics like Martin (1999), EDM's lack of an identifiable origin created a music culture that transcended race, class and gender barriers found elsewhere in popular music, youth culture and western society generally. For others, EDM's apolitical nature coupled with rave's hedonistic practices led to rave culture's decline. Unlike rap music, which articulates 'the pleasures and problems of black urban life in contemporary America' (Rose 1994: 2), EDM is virtually lyricless and thus is often categorized as 'music that's oriented toward impact rather than affect' (Reynolds 1998: 91). Music journalist Simon Reynolds was already proclaiming that 'the rave myth of transracial, cross-class unity [lay] in tatters' (86).

My interviews with women DJs reflect Reynolds' sentiment. None of them claims to have been drawn to the art of DJing by a particular political agenda. This is not to say their actions as DJs are not political, but rather that they do not view activism as part of their mission as DJs. If activism was their primary goal they might have turned instead to politically conscious rapping[1] or beyond music to documentary film-making or blogging.

Yet despite their apolitical stance, once they become DJs women are confronted with questions related to identity and representation, many of which are unique to their sex and gender and are therefore political in nature. Besides deciding what kind of music to invest in – financially and emotionally – and working to perfect their craft, they are immediately faced with other decisions that have little or nothing to do with their interest in music and DJing. They must decide on a DJ name, grapple with what to wear to gigs and come to terms with the extent to which they can (or cannot) control their stage identities. As women in a male-dominated, heterosexist industry, their physicality is constantly implicated in their EDM efforts in ways not necessarily experienced by men. Conversations with women DJs reveal the myriad ways in which they wrestle with their individual identities as both DJs/producers and women, even as they argue that gender is not an issue.

This chapter will explore the range of identities available to women DJs and the ways in which they publicly negotiate these identities. My interviews with women DJs provide answers to such key questions as: what kinds of images of female DJs are circulated in EDM outlets and popular culture more generally? How do these images impact women DJs and the ways in which they negotiate their stage personas? Finally, what concerns do these women express about issues related to identity and representation, and what role if any do these concerns play in their choice of DJ names?

In answering these questions, this chapter begins by briefly situating participants in a post-feminist cultural context in which DJs have become commodities. It then moves to an in-depth look at the identity categories available to women DJs. I conclude with a brief discussion of naming in DJ culture.

The (in)significance of feminism

Despite admitting that she is sometimes confronted with roadblocks, the internationally known techno DJ/producer Misstress Barbara, based in Montreal, Canada, glosses over the detours necessitated by her sex and gender. In her own words, 'I take the back door and I get there anyway, and then I end up getting all my respect' (Wehner 2000). When asked about the impact of being a woman in an overwhelmingly male business, she insists that 'it's time to leave this subject [of gender inequity] alone and move on' (Wehner 2000). Her post-feminist sentiments echo a trend in western culture over the past three decades that stems from the 1980s media backlash against the feminist movement (Faludi 1991; Douglas 1995). They reflect as well young women's refusal to view themselves or be seen by others as constrained by an unequal, patriarchal system.

Since 2000, Misstress Barbara has played clubs in countries worldwide, including Holland, Spain, Madrid, Slovenia, Italy and Malaysia. As one of the very few women to gain superstar status as a DJ/producer she can write off her gender as a non-issue, despite acknowledging the need to take the back door to gain respect, and despite critics who comment on her physical appearance as frequently as her music. In her book *Feminine Endings*, which fuses musicological and feminist concerns, Susan McClary (1991) argues that 'many superb women composers insist on making their gender identities a nonissue, precisely because there still remain so many essentialist assumptions about what music by women "ought" to sound like' (19). Perhaps Misstress Barbara can write off gender because she produces techno music, a subgenre of EDM that is particularly masculinized by its industrial sounds. Yet a review of her 2006 album *Come With Me* refers to her physical appearance, noting that 'Among the 17 tracks offered, we have to note the presence of 2 compositions by the beautiful 30 years [sic] old Sicilian' (anonymous reviewer at http://www.musicomania.ca/en/2006_albums.htm#Misstress%20Barbara). Consequently, despite her desire to make her gender a non-issue, it is still an undeniable influence on the EDM press.

Many of the women DJs interviewed for this project expressed views similar to those of Misstress Barbara. Even when discussing issues they were forced to deal with because they were women, interviewees consistently claimed an ability to rise above the constraints of sexual politics. This lack of critical inquiry on the part of some women DJs as to why they encounter gender-specific obstacles unfortunately sustains the very practices that disadvantage women.

I now turn to a brief overview of feminism and the backlash against it to contextually situate the lack of any explicit feminist politics today on the part of most young women in general and DJs in particular. Henry (2004) traces the first use of the term 'feminism' to 1919, when it was used by a women's literary group to assert that '[w]e're interested in people now – not in men and women' (Cott 1987, cited in Henry 2004: 19). Women nowadays easily identify with this perspective, despite the diversity of contemporary feminist views, as it draws on an appealing rhetoric of 'choice' and 'empowerment' parading under the banner of 'freedom' (McRobbie 2009). They tend not to identify with feminism or consider the challenges they face as gender-specific because to do so would be to acknowledge the continuation of sexist practices, the existence of which the backlash has worked diligently to refute. Young women today are rarely encouraged to rally for common causes in ways they were persuaded to organize during the second wave feminism movement of the 1970s, when women formed consciousness-raising groups to provide a space in which to discuss their lives and feelings and discover shared experiences. In these groups women raised awareness of the larger system of sexist practices of which they were a part (Dicker and Piepmeier 2003).

Presently, the social activism and radical politics of the second wave seem to be long forgotten despite the myriad ways in which women today benefit from the rights women fought for and won during the second wave (McRobbie 2009). Instead, carrying on with backlash practices that have been in place since the early 1980s, mass-mediated representations of feminism continue to portray it as fuelled by anger and hostility towards men. The underlying premise of the backlash against feminism – that 'women are enslaved by their own liberation' (Faludi 1991, cited in Braithwaite 2004: 22) – attributed women's supposed unhappiness to feminism's success (Faludi 1991; Douglas 1995, 2010). Dovetailing with the backlash, the term 'post-feminism' also entered the popular consciousness at this time, appearing in magazines such as *Newsweek* and *Time* to indicate both a rejection of feminism, implying its failure, as well as a time in which feminism is no longer necessary, signifying its success (Braithwaite 2004; Henry 2004). In either case, these rhetorical moves succeeded in establishing in the popular consciousness an image of feminism that is restrictive and ironically oppressive to women. Angela McRobbie (2009) argues that feminism has now been replaced with 'post-feminist substitutes from within the new hyper-visible consumer culture' (26). Correspondingly, Susan Douglas (2010) contends that the root of 'post-feminist' thinking is 'good, old-fashioned, grade-A sexism that reinforces good, old-fashioned, grade-A patriarchy. It's just much better disguised, in seductive Manolo Blahniks and an Ipex bra' (10). Sexism today is more nuanced, she argues, but just as pervasive as in the past.

Living in a media-saturated culture imbued with post-feminist discourse, it is understandable that women DJs in the United States generally discuss their individual efforts and strategies for overcoming barriers while dismissing all talk of structural inequalities. For despite the persistence of gender inequalities in EDM, these women live in a culture in which feminism is seen as unfashionable, passé and alienating. Nonetheless, I have chosen to use feminism as a critical framework throughout this book because I believe that doing so can facilitate an ideological shift allowing these women greater agency in their work and hopefully also in their personal lives. Additionally, though they choose not to refer to it as such, the perspectives, discourses and actions of female DJs speak often to feminist concerns and objectives.

For starters, the need to choose between two clearly defined approaches – presenting oneself as a woman first and DJ second or vice versa – does not apply to men. EDM DJs and fans alike assume that men are on stage because of their DJing abilities but when women are on stage, there is an implicit question about whether they are there because of their DJing abilities or because of their looks. The view held by most of the women I interviewed is reminiscent of the style of some feminists in the 1970s and 1980s, who sought to look as 'normal' and 'natural' as possible. In other words, they opted not to wear make-up, high heels or other clothing and accessories that they felt sexualized them. For women DJs today, this translates to a preference for not wearing 'stage clothes' (Bayton 1998: 108). Even though most of them do not present an overtly feminist agenda, most of them believe in presenting themselves as musicians first, women second and not as sex objects. As such, they do not endorse wearing provocative clothing on stage for their audience's pleasure.

The problem for women, Bayton suggests, is that 'however the performer dresses, she is making some sort of statement' (108). Women have traditionally been objects of the male gaze, so issues related to image and performance do not carry the same weight for men. Moreover, men may treat women differently if they believe women are using their sexuality to further their DJ agendas. In spite of their claims that they are freely choosing a personal style or look, the identities women DJs adopt tend to fit into one or more of three categories: 'sex kitten', 't-shirt DJ' and 'dyke'.

Since the explosion of EDM beginning in the late 1980s, DJ and club culture have become increasingly commercialized and motivated by profit margins, creating an environment that values predictable, marketable images. In today's celebrity-obsessed culture, the most successful DJs have become celebrities in their own right; in a modern twist, individuals who were celebrities first – including super models – have become DJs themselves. Given the importance of image, fitting into a range of known identities is paramount for all DJs but especially for women because of their outsider status in DJ culture.

Branding

The creation of a DJ's identity is closely related to the practice of branding. In an article about the inner workings of the British dance music industry, David Hesmondhalgh

(1998) argues that 'the notion of "branding" is a useful one in understanding the relationships between independent record companies and major corporations' (235). Independent record labels have always released the majority of EDM produced. In the 1980s and 1990s, these companies invested little in their artists/producers because labels and connoisseurs focused on 'shifts in style rather than on the identity of performers' (238). In other words, connoisseurs were more likely to consume certain subgenres as opposed to following specific artists. Within this model, record labels are the branded image, as opposed to the producers or DJs.

Ott and Herman (2003) connect this decentring of the artists to the unique characteristics of raves, which they describe as 'an ensemble performance involving the interaction of music, DJ, and ravers, in which no element is more or less important than the rest' (256). Quoting Gaillot (1999), they emphasize the anonymity of rave DJs, who did not perform onstage, were not introduced and were rarely recognized with applause at the end of their sets. However, as the popularity of rave culture grew in the United States in the 1990s, the music industry could no longer ignore the potential profits it represented (Ott and Herman 2003). In an effort to increase profits promoters began to heavily promote headlining DJs as the main event on flyers and in the rave space itself where it became increasingly common for DJs to perform on elevated stages not unlike rock bands, who typically play on raised stages where they are separated from their audience.

In the post-rave environment of the 2000s, official club events replaced illegal rave parties and DJs turned into celebrities as EDM events increasingly became 'superstar one-offs' (Anderson 2009). Anderson describes these occurrences as 'one time parties showcasing a main act or "star"', whose 'reputation and style help shape the event's organization, marketing, vibe, and identity' (44). Hesmondhalgh (1998) predicted this move by grasping early on the gradual undermining of the politics of anonymity in favour of the star system. While he discusses producers, the logic applies equally, if not more, to DJs. Turning EDM producers and DJs into brands favours the logic of capital accumulation. In Hesmondhalgh's words,

> groups and artists act as brand names for music and the fruits of promotional work can be transferred beyond one record to a series, as audiences carry certain expectations about sounds and messages from one record to the next. In addition, albums by established stars can be sold as 'back catalogue', a source of income which has become much more significant as the multi-media environment of the late twentieth century offers more and more opportunities for copyright owners.
>
> (247)

The practice of branding also benefits event promoters and club owners. In the case of the DJ, increasing commercialism creates a definite shift in power dynamics. Ott and Herman (2003) point out that the move from illegal rave spaces to legitimate clubs provided club personnel with a certain power over attendees, who were now seen as customers who must follow rules of acceptable behaviour. Similarly, the move to clubs decreased DJs' opportunities for gigs, making them more dependent on club owners and event promoters for income and exposure.

Those who have benefited from the auteur status granted to select DJs and producers are overwhelmingly men, whose fame and fortune has turned them into celebrities in their own right. A case in point is Richie Hawtin. A white English-Canadian techno producer/DJ, Hawtin moved from England to Windsor, Canada at age nine. By 17 he was playing in Detroit clubs, part of the second wave of techno artists in the Detroit area. He co-founded the record label Plus 8 with John Acquaviva in the early 1990s and began producing minimal techno tracks, which he released under the moniker Plastikman.

Hawtin is one of the few producers whose stylistic approach has carried over well beyond his music to every element of his public persona, including his record labels, stage presence and the Plastikman logo itself, a minimal image of a dancing character. The pervasiveness of Hawtin's self-branding can be measured by the number of people sporting Plastikman tattoos at EDM events, the presence of the logo on the website www. brandsoftheworld. com and the Canadian Design Resource's statement that 'Today [the Plastikman logo] is synonymous not only with Hawtin's music, but with electronic music in general' (Erdmann 2006 at http://www.canadiandesignresource.ca/officialgallery/logo/plastikman-logo/).

One additional factor Hesmondhalgh (1998) cites for EDM's increasing commercialization since the mid-1990s is its newer audiences' desire for the music to be recognized by the masses in ways that can be achieved only via the star system (248). This change, which has been described as a shift from 'communion to commodity spectacle' (Ott and Herman 2003: 259), has significant implications for DJs – especially women DJs. Inside

Figure 2.1: Plastikman logo by Ron Cameron. Courtesy of Minus Inc.

the club the DJ is positioned as the main event or star, showcased onstage and visible for all to see. As DJs began to take on star status, the importance of a DJ's physical image was heightened. As is the case with rock bands, bookings then grew increasingly dependent on a combination of skills *and* image. In this context, having a recognizable brand helps DJs stand out from their competition, which in an increasingly hyper-competitive DJ market has become more and more important over the years.

DJs, supermodels and celebrities

The importance of image in DJ culture is reflected in its ties to celebrity and consumer culture. Since the 1990s DJs have been hailed as popular musicians on a par with rock stars. Some critics have even gone so far as to claim that DJs have 'replaced supermodels as the new "hot" celebrities' (Reighley 2000, cited in Ott and Herman 2003: 263). In fact, they are often one and the same. Contributing to this viewpoint is the increased presence of female models posing as DJs in print advertisements and television commercials to sell products such as candy bars, face wash, computers and Vitaminwater.

The changes to music technologies, the explosion of DJ culture and the increase in the number of women EDM DJs have been a double-edged sword for DJs, especially women. In the past EDM connoisseurs had to spend a great deal of time and money searching for cutting-edge music produced on vinyl and sold in specialty record shops. Today, MP3s can be downloaded in seconds. While there is more to being a good DJ than amassing a record collection, the ease with which MP3s can be downloaded has created a climate in which anyone with an iPod and Internet access, or simply a smart phone, can be a sort of DJ. In cities like New York, these changes have had profound effects on DJ culture of all types, including limiting opportunities for women like those interviewed for this project.

Unlike the 1990s and early 2000s – the time period in which many of the women I interviewed took up DJing – today corporations and dance clubs are increasingly hiring young (under age 25) celebrities and models (both male and female) as DJs, despite their limited experience or skills and without regard to their musical interests. Club owners are primarily concerned with generating profit. In a celebrity-obsessed culture, the presence of a supermodel/celebrity as the main event/spectacle, as opposed to a lesser-known DJ with more talent, is much more likely to draw not only a crowd, but the *right* crowd. An article in *W* magazine titled 'Invasion of the Dilettante DJs' sums up the phenomenon, noting, 'DJing – and the visibility that goes with it – has replaced handbag designing as the go-to profession for It girls and boys' (Thompson 2009: 106).

The decreasing distinction between models/celebrities and DJs has exacerbated the pressure on female DJs in particular to conform to heterosexual, hyper-feminized images. One example of the favouring of sex/celebrity over skill is model-turned-DJ Harley Viera-Newton. The daughter of a record executive, Harley is a Brazilian celebrity under contract with Elite modeling agency; she is also the house DJ for the top fashion house Christian

Dior (Thompson 2009). Celebrity DJs like Viera-Newton and Alexandra Richards (daughter of Rolling Stones guitarist Keith Richards) earn upwards of $10,000 per gig, compared to $250–$400 for non-celebrities (Thompson 2009: 108).

These examples illustrate the changing role of the DJ in the twenty-first century, where *who* is DJing increasingly matters more than the 'what' and 'how well'. This reverses the trend of the 1980s and 1990s, when DJs were redefined as technological and musical virtuosos to build up their importance and celebrity status. In my research, three main female DJ categories emerged regarding appearance: sex kitten, t-shirt DJ and dyke. The following sections exam each category and DJs' varied responses to this cultural shift from a focus on musical virtuosity to an obsession with image.

Sex kitten

I use the term 'sex kitten' to refer to women whose image conforms to heterosexist beauty standards (such as being thin and having long hair) and who are sexually provocative, wearing tight and/or revealing clothing. The dichotomy that heterosexual female DJs in particular struggle with – to be t-shirt DJs or sex kittens – arises from the environment in which DJs pursue paid gigs. In the paragraphs that follow I first address images of women DJs in popular culture and the popular press, then link these images with commercial music culture and the role of branding.

Several of the DJs I interviewed mentioned DJ Portia Surreal as an extreme example of the 'sex kitten' image. In the mid-2000s, the front page of the New York City-based DJ's website www.portiasurreal.com featured a busty Portia posing in sexy lingerie, with a caption that read, 'Erotic Fetish DJ Extraordinaire'. According to her booking agency XlMusic's website:

> Portia debuted in 2002 as the first ever Erotic Fetish Burlesque DJ for a lingerie themed glam club event entitled: SEXXXY. Turntables suspended from a ceiling above a lavish fur bed and an evening of ecstatic erotica was where the heated passion of Surreal's Disc Jockey Burlesque first became introduced. This magical night launched a world-wide mass response ... With the overnight success of her charismatic novelty, Portia was named as one of the newest up and coming dj's in 2003 by BPM Magazine. Within one year of the 'topless' celebration Portia began performing for leading club varieties and headlined with Tiesto at the Rubber Pimp N Ho Ball for over 7000 people. With her self attained notoriety, Portia has successfully surpassed patron attendance records at numerous large scale venues as a solo headlining act ... She has been featured in numerous accredited magazines such as: Spin, Maxim, FHM, King, Skin Two, Playboy, and Hustler, as well as The Fetish Magazine Marquis, who declared her the 'World's number 1 Erotic DJ' in 2004.
> (http://www.xlmusic.gr/modern/xlmusic_djs/international_djs_and_
> artists/34/dj_portia_surreal.scratch#more-34)

In 2009, the primary web presence for DJ Portia Surreal's 'Erotic DJ Showgirl' was located on MySpace, while her previous URL www.portiasurreal.com hosted a pornography website. At the time I am writing this in 2011, her MySpace page is blank but videos of her burlesque DJ show from the mid-2000s can be easily accessed online.

DJ Portia Surreal's popularity coincided with a pictorial in the April 2004 issue of *Playboy* magazine titled 'Beauty and the Beat: Seven Sexy DJs Spin Out of Their Clothes on Our Dance Floor. They've Got Grooves.' The six-page spread includes little text other than an introduction and brief captions for the women featured, along with a quote from each of them. The introduction claims, 'Whether they specialize in techno, tribal, house, hip hop, retro or electro, these girls all rock – and think it's fine if sex appeal is part of what's raising the temperature on the dance floor.' Readers are told, 'one mix minx, DJ Tuesdae, even spins topless' and proclaims herself 'a press whore' (72).

The pages that follow include two pictures of each featured DJ. One of the photos shows each woman in a tank top – with the exception of DJ Tuesdae, who is featured in a bra – as she spins. A larger image of each DJ features her topless, with little clothing from the waist down. In none of these pictures are the DJs actually DJing. The only clue that these women are DJs are the images of DJ Tatiana and DJ Snezana featuring headphones in the shots, and possibly the picture of DJ Ines sitting on a full (closed) record box in a dark alley. For the most part the DJs simply pose suggestively on tabletops, bars and railings. The lack of any discussion of music in the spread speaks volumes about what readers should find entertaining about these women: not their talent, but instead the titillation that results from objectifying their bodies.

DJ Rap

For the most part, DJ Portia Surreal is seen as a novelty and the DJs featured in the April 2004 issue of *Playboy* remain mostly anonymous in EDM culture. One woman who has managed to attain fame and graces the cover of numerous EDM magazines is Britain's DJ Rap [Charrisa Saverio], who secured her first record deal with Sony Music in 1999 (www.djrap.com). Marketed as someone whose work defies conventional genres, she is principally known as a drum and bass DJ/producer. The June 1999 issue of *CMJ New Music Monthly* featured DJ Rap on its cover. In a review of the press coverage, a critic at *Pinknoises. com*[2] argued that 'the magazine – with Saverio's jaunty blessing – sells an intuitive story of a pop musician (written by a classily disinterested gay man) using the tried-and-true *Maxim* rule: 15% of the cover should comprise cleavage' (Siegler 2002).

That same year DJ Rap was also featured in 'The Girly Issue' of Chicago EDM magazine *Velocity: Accelerated Culture*. Alongside the interview text is a long shot of DJ Rap dressed in black, wearing high heels and a seductive expression on her face (see Figure 2.2). The number one reason the magazine cites for loving DJ Rap is that 'she gives us "the feeling,"' as expressed in the following statement:

One look at any of the countless heart-stopping pictures of Ms. Rap (Charrisa Saverio) is more than enough evidence to try her case. What's the charge, you ask? Being absolutely gorgeous. Pretty even. DJ Rap is fine. Although that's hardly the only reason we dig Rap, it doesn't hurt that aesthetically, she's a perfect cross of both Jennifers, Lopez and Aniston. To sum it up in a word: Yummy!

As a tall blonde, DJ Rap is capable of easily adopting the 'sex kitten' identity category. Physically she embodies the characteristics the mass media teaches women to embrace and men to desire.

When asked about the release of her first artist album *Learning Curve* (1999) by Sony subsidiary Higher Ground, she stated, 'This is a pop record … anyone on the scene that I've grown up with knows that this is what I've wanted to do from day one. They all know I've always wanted a band' (Sterling 1999: 48). More than a decade after *Learning Curve*'s release DJ Rap has yet to achieve her dream of being in a band, but her rhetorical strategy has been successful. Because she claimed that becoming or remaining an EDM producer was not her goal, it is difficult for those within EDM culture to label DJ Rap a sellout,

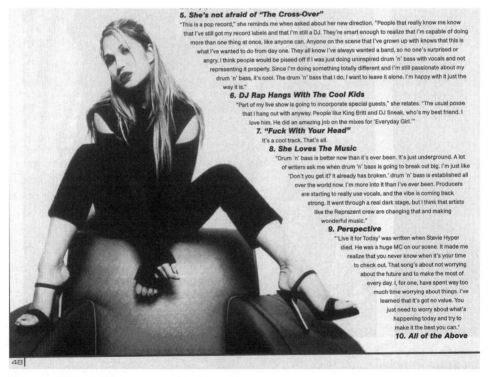

Figure 2.2: DJ Rap in *Velocity* magazine (1999).

despite her appearance in a Twix candy bar commercial in 2003 and her embodiment, in mass-mediated contexts, of the 'sex kitten' persona from which so many women DJs work to distance themselves. Yet, regardless of her claims in *Velocity*, she has invested a great deal of time and energy in her career as an EDM artist, and even had a guest DJ page on the now defunct *Sister SF* website, which suggests some interest in being recognized among EDM connoisseurs.

Based on her mass-mediated images it is tempting to simply categorize DJ Rap as a 'sex kitten' DJ; however, the persona she represents on stage is at times strikingly different from these images. Headlining the all-female DJ event in San Francisco in 2005 that I describe in some detail in the introduction to Chapter 4, her look was quite casual as she appeared on stage in a t-shirt and jeans. In fact, in person on this night she bore very little resemblance whatsoever to her numerous mass-mediated representations. In this context her adoption of the 't-shirt DJ' persona for the night fit right in with the other female DJs performing. DJ Rap's choice to strategically use her sexuality to promote herself is emblematic of a central tenet of third wave feminism. Aiming to be inclusive and respectful of the choices women make, third-wavers believe that feminism is less about the specific choices women make and more about women acting with a 'feminist consciousness', defined as 'knowledge of what one is doing and why one is doing it' (Baumgardner and Richards 2000: 83, as cited in Snyder-Hall 2010: 255).

On the one hand, DJ Rap's success can be seen as an inspiration to women in EDM. However, *Velocity*'s rhetorical strategy of positioning her alongside the Jennifers – Aniston and Lopez – all but removes her from EDM culture, as it represents both the Hollywood success that is unattainable for all but a few, and an image that many women in EDM cannot or chose not to embody. It was clear from my interviews that the majority of the women interviewed for this project felt a divide between themselves and the 'sex kitten' persona. Most likely DJ Rap is aware of these sentiments and thus chooses to use her sexuality strategically. Without a doubt it has facilitated her international success as a DJ and producer. Of the DJs I interviewed, DJ Icon [Connie Wong] makes use of these strategies in her construction of her DJ persona more so than the others.

DJ Icon

DJ Icon [Connie Wong] started DJing in San Francisco in 1997 and had her first out-of-town booking in 1999. In 2001 she moved to New York City and held a DJ residency at the popular nightclub Limelight before returning to San Francisco in 2003. In a 2003 interview DJ Icon observed, 'The female DJ thing is fairly new, but not new anymore. Now all the novelty has worn off. It used to be, "Wow, let's go see them because female DJs are hot." Now lots of us are professionals with robust careers.' Despite the fact that in the mid-2000s San Francisco had the highest concentration of women DJs in the United States, she added:

It's still difficult getting the respect that a male DJ would get. It's gotten a lot better [than it used to be] but people still have a hard time taking us seriously. They think we only get booked because we're female, or for the way we look … and completely discount the fact that we actually have talent, despite our looks. It used to bother me but it doesn't matter what they think. If promoters are booking me on account of that prejudice, I'm just going to show up proud, play well, and show them that their prejudice is wrong. I pretty much win either way.

(DJ Icon, 20 June 2003 interview)

In many ways her perspective echoes those of other women DJs; however, DJ Icon's confidence in both her DJ skills and her stage persona is striking. Because of her confidence and interest in fashion along with her body type – she is a petite Asian-American – DJ Icon's stage persona is somewhat versatile. Photos on her website www.djicon.com show her DJing at times in a t-shirt and jeans, but on other occasions she dresses more provocatively.

DJ Icon was featured in a documentary about 12 up-and-coming DJs on the Showtime network that caught the eye of an MTV talent scout, who then cast her as the DJ on the internationally syndicated, 25-episode MTV™ series 'The Wade Robson Project', a talent search competition for hip hop dancers. In the final edits of the episodes DJ Icon is positioned behind a set of turntables, where she spends most of her screen time standing in the background and not DJing. Clearly, MTV was more interested in DJ Icon as a novelty than as a DJ who would contribute to the show in a substantive way. She explained that she was hesitant to take on the role because she knew that it could potentially harm her image, but in fact, it opened many doors, such as being signed to Chaotica Music Agency, one of the biggest agencies of that time, who managed many top-tiered artists such as Daft Punk, Chemical Brothers, Paul Oakenfold, Sandra Collins and more.

Since that time she has worked diligently to create a branded identity for herself. It is clear from her polished website that she understands and values the importance of image. The site features several videos and hundreds of pictures of her under the heading 'DJ action shots' and includes a separate section of 'press shots'. The press shots are further broken down into two categories: 'older press shots' from 2003 and 'new rockstar shots'[3] from 2010. While the older set credits only a photographer, the new set also credits make up, hair and clothing stylists. In addition to looking more professional, the newer pictures feature a sexier DJ Icon (see Figure 2.3). In neither set of pictures are there any clues that these are photos of a DJ. However, the 'DJ action shots' section of the site features dozens of photos of DJ Icon using DJ equipment and similar to DJ Rap's onstage persona; in these shots her dress and style is more casual.

Other sections and headings on the comprehensive website include info, music, events and a blog. The events page reveals an active DJ schedule for 2010, with gigs in Germany, the United Kingdom and cities across the United States. In addition to her personal website she also has a profile on MySpace, where she has 59,471 friends, and on Facebook, where

Figure 2.3: DJ Icon (2009). Copyright Jeff Steinmetz, rockstarshots.com

she has 3374 fans. Additionally, she has 1570 Twitter followers. These numbers from 2011 are remarkable for an EDM DJ. Similar to DJ Rap, through her choice to strategically embody a sexy or provocative image and engage in marketing tactics similar to those used by artists in other parts of the music industry, DJ Icon has created a successful brand for herself. Strategically embodying this persona presumably has helped her maintain her active DJ schedule, because one's image has become ever more important since the women interviewed here first began DJing in the 1990s and early 2000s.

T-shirt DJs

The most prominent theme to emerge from my interviews with women DJs is their fear of being perceived as sex kittens. These concerns and their efforts *not* to be viewed in this light are understandable given the ways DJs have typically been depicted in EDM culture. Chapter 1 illustrated how DJs have been rhetorically positioned as patriarchal, musical superheroes. With male DJs controlling and dominating the crowd, women are generally viewed as passive participants or, as Herman (2006) observed, as 'merely the *angel[s] in the club* – powerless over their lust for the big (name) DJ' (29, emphasis added).

Herman's use of the term 'angels' to label female club goers is suggestive not only of women's role in club spaces but in western culture more broadly. America's largest lingerie retailer Victoria Secret employs the term to refer to its spokeswomen and fashion show models. There is also the *Charlie's Angels* media franchise and the countless references to angels in Japanese animation. In all of these cases the so-called angels are hypersexualized personas created to cater to heterosexual male titillation. Thus, to describe women in the club space as angels further reinforces their position not only as hypersexual, docile bodies, at the mercy of the DJ but also as spectacle for the male gaze. Remarking on the highly sexual dress and appearance of raver girls in the United Kingdom in the 1990s Angela McRobbie (1994) notes that to some extent this hypersexual appearance is 'symbolically sealed or "closed off" through the dummy, the whistle, or the ice lolly' (168). In other words, the culture created an environment in which rave accoutrements such as pacifiers, whistles, candy and popsicles literally and symbolically silenced partygoers. McRobbie sees these actions as specifically problematic for women because their silence worked to further enforce the idea that their purpose was to be seen and not heard. Although these oral devices have disappeared in the post-rave environment, the hypersexualized images have mostly intensified.

Accordingly, women continue to struggle with how to promote themselves and their work as EDM DJs. DJ Barbarella [Barbara Mayers] of San Diego, California identified two schools of thought about how a DJ presents herself. 'You can be a novelty item, have no talent, wear a bikini and make a lot of money', or, as she herself has done, 'always wear a long-sleeved Adidas t-shirt because I don't like being objectified at all' (23 May 2003 interview). Male DJs tend to wear t-shirts and jeans onstage. Thus, in the minds of most of the women I interviewed, adopting this standard wardrobe helps ensure that they are onstage because of their DJ skills and not because of their sex – at least not exclusively.

Some of the women interviewed believed being female had benefitted their careers, but not because they presented themselves as sex kittens. One such woman is San Francisco Bay Area DJ Denise [Denise Rees], one of the few women I interviewed, who earns a living solely from her EDM efforts.

> I've actually just found it if anything to have been a benefit for me to be a girl just because of San Francisco, which is a liberal place. It's hard to say, I think it's just with the whole thing with there not being as [many] female DJs as there are guys. You're almost a rare thing to be watching and some people do want to come out and watch you play, especially if you're good or have big boobs I guess, which I don't so I must fit the other category.
>
> (8 July 2003 interview)

DJ Denise's comments mirror those of other interviewees who believe that being a woman in a male-dominated scene can be an advantage because it can pique people's curiosity. She also believes women can be booked either for their skill or for conforming to the sex kitten persona. DJ Denise is a petite Asian-American woman with short dark hair and usually wears t-shirts or other loose-fitting clothing to gigs, so she clearly has not chosen to present herself as a sexual spectacle. However, even though she does not assume a sex kitten identity, her physical appearance and style still fit within the range of looks considered acceptable within EDM culture.

The dichotomy that DJ Denise and others identify is problematic because it assumes that a woman can be either a sex kitten or a good DJ, but never both. Such reasoning places further pressure on women already wrestling with how to represent themselves in an environment where being too feminine can affect their credibility as good DJs. DJ Aura [Tina Nerpio] from San Jose, California is the only other Asian-American DJ I interviewed. She believes that many Bay Area promoters book women to entice heterosexual men to their events:

> I don't think that promoters look at the woman as a musical artist. They're more like, 'If I get her maybe more guys will come.' They only get one lady DJ out of like ten guys so that's how I see it right now. I don't see a lot of girls getting hired unless they really know people or if they have been doing it for a while and they have connections.
>
> (18 June 2003 interview)

DJ Aura's comments imply a degree of mistrust of most promoters. The uneasiness women feel about working with promoters and club management whose intentions are unknown has drawn some women to create viable EDM networks with other women. This phenomenon is further addressed in Chapters 3 and 4.

Figure 2.4: DJ Denise in San Francisco (2003).

DJ Aura's and DJ Denise's observations led me to ask women if they feel pressured to conform to the 'sex kitten' identity when performing. Most women said they do not feel pressured to do so despite the fact that doing so could potentially increase their visibility and lead to more bookings. In her study of women in rock, Mavis Bayton (1998) argues that 'dressing for the stage cannot be completely "innocent" or spontaneous since it always involves some deliberation' (107). Thus the decision to look 'natural' is always a strategic choice. The women in San Francisco credited the liberal atmosphere of the Bay Area as a possible reason for not feeling pressured to look a certain way, again even though doing so could boost their DJ careers. They would rather abide by their principles than adopt a stage persona with which they are not comfortable even if the end result is a less successful DJ career in but especially beyond the San Francisco Bay Area. In addition to their geographical location, that the women interviewed had day jobs and other income streams gave them more freedom in making these decisions. Despite this freedom, even their chosen look tends to fit into one of the identity categories outlined in this chapter.

Psychedelic-trance[4] DJ KT [Katie Pollard] suggests that subgenres, and by extension sub-scenes, are one possible explanation for the conformity as well as the variations in women DJs' identities.

I think most of the women here do what they would normally do. The people who like to be hot mammas are a hot mamma when they're DJing, and the people who show up in a long sleeve t-shirt wear that all the time. Everyone's – male or female – stage presence is a component of being a DJ. It depends on what scene you're in. In some scenes the aesthetic is not a lot of lighting, dark, big speakers, anonymous DJ – you just see the headphones and a little glow coming off the mixer and you're not even sure who it is up there, the music's just coming from God or something. I've been to parties like that and I actually kind of like that, that aesthetic. As a dancer it's not about the DJ, it's about the music … we do a lot of decorating at the parties with tapestries and stuff. The eye candy isn't always the DJ.

(18 June 2005 interview)

DJ KT's comment suggests that specific subgenres can dictate not only the kind of music a DJ spins, but also the venues chosen for events and the personas DJs adopt.

The psychedelic-trance (psy-trance) community in San Francisco, to which DJ KT belongs, is more countercultural than most other EDM scenes. It receives little coverage in the EDM press and does not figure prominently in EDM histories because it evolved in the late 1990s, much later than other kinds of EDM. In addition, based on my observations of psy-trance events in San Francisco, the scene seems to attract a relatively older crowd, with many participants in their late 20s and 30s.

Unlike the shiny and provocative clothing dancers tend to wear in trendy dance clubs, psy-trancers of both sexes often prefer the baggy clothes, dreadlocks and dyed hair more reminiscent of 'deadheads' than clubbers. To some extent this style carries over from trance music's origins among the hippies who relocated to Goa, India in the 1960s. Reminiscent of the early days of rave culture, in the psy-trance scene DJs are only one part of the entire event experience, not the central focal point as they are at most post-rave DJ events. Katie's reference to DJs as 'eye candy' alludes to her awareness that in more commercial EDM scenes, women DJs are often depicted foremost as visual – as opposed to aural – spectacles.

Along similar lines, DJ Ara [Heather Reagan] talked about her choice to wear whatever is comfortable. She was hesitant and clearly uncomfortable discussing the subject of whether women get gigs because of their sex. Yet ultimately she sided with DJ Denise in concluding that sometimes being a woman can be helpful.

I don't know if it's for the wrong reason. People look at my picture and say, 'Oh, she's cute.' I've had people e-mail and tell me they like my picture and I'm like, 'OK, you wanna hear my music first and then tell me if you like me?' It's odd. It's weird because do I be offended or get defensive or say, 'Well, it's what got me in the door'? If you think I'm cute and that's why you want me, let me show you my music and then I'll really rock your world. That's happened and I've really felt good about that but then at the same time I felt bad because that's not right to say, 'Oh, we need a girl, you're cute, come on' … I certainly would never play anywhere where they ask me to wear certain things.

(20 June 2003 interview)

DJ Ara's assertion that she would never agree to 'wear certain things' undoubtedly refers to her decision not to embody a sex kitten persona or be treated as obvious 'eye candy'.

Several women discussed their DJ identities as extensions of who they are and how they present themselves offstage. Conversations with DJ Amber [Amber Nixon] further illuminated the complex choices female DJs must make.

I don't really hold myself or present myself in a way that would give someone a message that I'm due to be treated differently. It's the way you carry yourself. It's how the marketing materials you send out look. I've only recently gotten comfortable with putting my picture on something [see Figure 2.6]. Now I've gotten professional enough that I can step back

Figure 2.5: Cover art for DJ Amber's Mix CD 'Gold' (2002). Designer: Rob Andreoli.

Figure 2.6: Cover art for DJ Amber's Mix CD 'neo.maximal' (2010).
Designer: Patrick Farley.

and see that me putting myself on the front is beneficial and it's not me sending a message saying, 'Oh, I'm so super great', or saying, 'Look at my face, not my music.' I have sort of let go of being worried of sending that message. It's totally normal and standard for a picture of the artist to appear on the cover of a CD, it's totally normal industry wide and I'm at peace with that now. When I pick what pictures and things I wanna put up, there can't be a promo picture of me that's racy because I never really dress racy. It's really about how you looked at the time so I couldn't really make the choice so I'm gonna look how I'm gonna look. However, I do like to dress up but it's more because I like to put feathers and birds in my hair, and not because I'm like, 'Oh, look at me, I'm pretty.'

(16 July 2003 interview)

While DJ Amber does not claim to consistently wear t-shirts to gigs, her philosophy and DJ persona mesh with those of other t-shirt DJs in the sense that she is very concerned with not looking 'racy'. As a tall, thin, white redhead, DJ Amber could purposefully embody the sex kitten role to further her DJ career. As this passage indicates, she spent many years worried that a wrong PR move would mistakenly present her as such. It was only after establishing herself as a DJ for eight years in the local San Francisco scene that she felt comfortable including her picture on her mix CDs.

Dykes

In addition to the sex kitten and t-shirt DJ personas, a third image that surfaced during interviews was that of the 'dyke' DJ and it applies to women who first and foremost identify as lesbian. In most cases it manifests itself in physical appearance and applies to gay women who sport short haircuts and non-gender specific clothing. In fewer instances it represents identification with particular social and/or political stances in an effort to reclaim the once derogatory label. Significantly, the embodiment of a visible dyke identity in EDM culture can enable women to be more easily accepted in EDM culture because men do not consider them to have an unfair advantage in securing paid DJ gigs the way they might t-shirt DJs or sex kittens. Unfortunately, the EDM press can also position them as objectifiers, who embody a traditionally heterosexual male gaze, as in the case of superstar DJ Irene.

In July 2003 I attended a potluck in Portland, Oregon hosted by and for women DJs. This monthly event had been ongoing since 2001, primarily under the direction of Layla Dudley, a local DJ. She explained that the monthly meetings had led to the coordination of local DJ events everywhere from clubs to coffee shops. One of the women I spoke with at the potluck was Sappho [Megan Andricos], a self-identified lesbian and techno connoisseur. Sappho had short brown hair and a medium build, and wore baggy green cargo pants and a loose t-shirt to the meeting. Her clothing was similar to that of the t-shirt DJs described above but because she is gay and has a short haircut, male DJs view her differently from the t-shirt DJs. Men in the local scene, who typically were unsupportive of women DJs, gave her a lot of support.

> I got a lot of support from guys who don't normally support female DJs because I'm gay. They're like, 'You're not out there selling your sex.' I have one friend, he can be really mean toward female DJs. He's a DJ. I know it's jealousy. He's like, 'You're the coolest DJ I know.' He's gone and heckled women DJs when he's drunk.
>
> (13 July 2003 interview)

Sappho's comment suggests that not only are women judgmental of others whom they perceive as using their sex to advance their careers but so are men. Throughout my interviews women recounted stories of men not treating them as equals. Men often either assumed that they did not know how to use technology proficiently or would not extend to them typical DJ etiquette that then made them look inexperienced in front of an audience. For example, because there are variances between DJ set ups, it is customary for the DJ completing his or her set to briefly review the set up with the upcoming DJ. In several cases women complained that male DJs who preceded them did not extend to them this courtesy but instead let them fend for themselves. It is unclear whether male DJs acted this way because they looked down on female DJs and did not consider them serious competition or because they felt threatened by them, but what Sappho's story does demonstrate is that some men believe that because of their sex women have an unfair advantage when it comes to securing DJ gigs. Because of her physical appearance and sexual orientation, men in the local scene did not see Sappho as having an unfair advantage in advancing her DJ career and so they supported her.

EDM culture on a broader scale also supports dyke DJs. Based in Los Angeles, DJ Irene is a self-identified lesbian known as one of the bestselling DJs in the United States. Her bookings include the official Grammy after-party and the massive Coachella music festival in Indio, California. Most pictures of DJ Irene, including many of the covers of her DJ Mix CDs, include only a headshot that draws attention to her extremely short, bleached blonde hair, which is often styled in a mohawk. When she appears in long shots, DJ Irene looks androgynous in men's clothing. Similar to the reasons why male DJs in Portland extended their support to Sappho, it is understood that DJ Irene is popular because of her DJ skills and not her appearance or sexuality.

However, this is not to say that lesbian DJs, including DJ Irene, are never represented as primarily sexual beings rather than musical authors (Herman 2006). In his textual analysis of rave artefacts, Herman analysed a 2001 issue of *Mixer* – an EDM magazine targeted at fans – featuring DJ Irene, in which 'she commands the attention of five stereotypically gay men and four immodestly dressed women who are lustfully draped around her' (29). In this image, she is clearly sexualized as an object of desire.

Alternatively, the cover for her 2009 release *Dissonance* features her fully clothed, standing tall in a costume that includes a red cape, with a shirtless, sculpted male body on the floor to her right and a scantily clad, heavily tattooed woman in a cat-like pose to her left. Both are wearing chains around their necks and are presumably at her mercy. Thus, while her dyke status may desexualize her in the eyes of her male counterparts, at times DJ Irene is still presented as either a sexual object, as suggested in the former example, or in the latter case as an aggressive patriarchal figure, who objectifies others. In either case, sex is still a theme that competes with her musical productivity. For some DJs, working in a gay context is a way to avoid these trappings.

Hip hop dykes

Only one other DJ I interviewed self-identified as gay, and more specifically as a dyke. On the surface this seemed odd, given that many of the interviews were conducted in San Francisco, which is known for its thriving gay culture. However, during my interview with Melissa Burnell, who DJ's simply as Melissa, the reasons for this became clearer. The week before our interview I went to see her perform at the Cherry Bar in San Francisco. Upon entering the space two observations immediately struck me. The music pulsating from the speakers was not EDM but hip hop, and there were no men in the club aside from employees and the two friends who accompanied me. Instead, the room was packed with women, most of whom visibly embodied a dyke/butch persona. As Melissa explains:

> San Francisco especially is one of the few places that is still very separatist. My group of
> friends, the ones who own the bars and run the clubs, definitely don't consider themselves

lesbians as much as they do dykes, which is kind of a more in-your-face attitude. Lesbians tend to assimilate more whereas dykes want to stand out and be more noticeable, which you're fine to refer to me as. I actually prefer it.

(19 May 2005 interview)

Despite her verbal embodiment of a dyke identity, both on and off stage Melissa's style parallels that of Sappho and the heterosexual t-shirt DJs discussed above much more than that of DJ Irene. Melissa had long brown hair and wore a t-shirt and jeans the night she was DJing. On the day of our interview she traded her jeans for a knee-length skirt paired with casual sandals. Thus, for Melissa the embodiment of a 'dyke DJ' identity is much more associated with her political affinity and where she DJs than with how she dresses. Since moving to San Francisco in 1999 she established a name for herself in the local lesbian club scene with a club night she was part of called 'Brownie for My Bitches'. At the time of our interview in 2005, the intimate club night had been running on the second Tuesday of every month for four years. This is an impressive length of time for a monthly club night to survive, given the plethora of clubs in the city.

Melissa noted that she did not know a lot of straight hip hop DJs and thought that straight women primarily spin EDM. My research supports Melissa's casual observations. After being a hip hop DJ from 1992 to 2001, DJ Aura [Tina Nerpio] moved on to DJing house music. When asked what prompted her to cross over after so many years, she replied:

I like the crowd better; with hip hop it's a younger crowd, thuggish – dressed down, not really there [in clubs] to listen to the music. Anybody can listen to hip hop on the radio. With house, people really want to listen to the DJ.

(18 June 2003 interview)

DJ Aura's experience at straight hip hop venues in San Jose differed greatly from Melissa's involvement with hip hop nights at dyke clubs in San Francisco. She described why she and other dykes liked mainstream hip hop from the 2000s, despite its overt misogyny:

I think that [dykes] tend to think that the women hip hop talks about is not talking about them because they're not, the dykes, they're not girly girls. There's this one Dr. Dre song, there's this line where they're talking about someone's momma and they're dissin' them. The line is, 'I heard your momma was a Frisco dyke' and when I play that in the clubs the girls go crazy and like here it is this homophobic sexist statement that the dykes just, they feel like the song's about them. They're so excited it's like, you know, 'Oh he's talking about us, I'm a Frisco dyke'. So I think the girls just don't really think it applies to them or it's like, oh you know, sorta like, the reclaiming of the sexist attitude and being able to say it doesn't bother me. But they *love* the hip hop.

(19 May 2005 interview)

Melissa, who is white, and the women she spins hip hop for, who based on my fieldwork are also predominantly white, did not see themselves as implicated in hip hop's misogyny, because they are gay. Tricia Rose addresses this position in her book *Hip Hop Wars* (2008), which examines the state of the conversation on hip hop in the late 2000s. Similar to Melissa's fan base, Rose argues that it is common for women and girls to comply with hip hop's representation of women as bitches and hoes because they do not believe the rappers are talking about them, and therefore do not believe that such public, disempowering labels impact them. Rose's point is that such labeling is in fact hurtful to all women. Although Rose is speaking about black women, her argument is valid beyond the black community because sexist, denigrating labeling and other strategies that maintain male power are not confined to a particular race or class.

What's in a name?

A final element fundamental to DJ identities but more difficult to categorize along lines of sex, gender or sexuality is the art of naming in EDM culture. While some DJs and producers use their birth names, many others adopt alternate monikers for their artist profiles. The website dj.com boasts that it is the 'world's largest DJ directory', with hundreds of thousands of names registered at the site. The top ten DJs in June 2010 were: Tiesto, Armin van Burren, David Guetta, ATB, Deadmaus, Paul van Dyk, Above and Beyond, Ferry Cordsten, Carl Cox and Benny Benassi. All of them are men. Four of the names are clearly not birth names (Tiesto, ATB, Deadmaus and Above and Beyond) while the origins of the other six are less apparent.

The practice of adopting a stage name has become so common in EDM that several DJ name generators can be found online, including the BBC Cornwall's DJ name finder game. The introduction to the name generator reads:

> Every DJ needs a top stage name, and err Fergus Trelawney just might not have the necessary ring – but panic not … The BBC Cornwall website is coming to your rescue, with our new, and may we say rather marvellous, state-of-the-art DJ naming machine.
>
> (www.bbc.co.uk/cornwall/clubbing/quiz/quiz.shtml)

Upon entering my own name into the selector, I was presented with the name 'Sizzler Pasty-Babe'. The game is meant to be humorous and playful, but the existence of this and many other sites like it speaks not only to the prominent role of naming in EDM culture, but also its inherent sexism when a name that sounds feminine yields a result along the lines of 'Sizzler Pasty-Babe'.

Linguist Jannis K. Androutsopoulos (2001) has studied the relationship between names and musical style and concludes that 'names can be quite revealing about the ideology of a community or culture' (16). With respect to hip hop names, Androutsopoulos notes that it is common for newcomers to imitate the name of a successful band or artist. As an example he points to hip hop musician and DJ Grandmaster Flash, whose success prompted other artists to adopt forms of his name in addition to his musical style, for example, Grandmaster Caz and Grand Wizard Theodore.

Androutsopoulos (2001) also points out the links between DJ names and references to various elements of EDM culture, including futurism, space, science fiction, music/rhythm and hallucinogenic drugs. His examples include EDM artists Space Planet, the Orb, Future Sound of London and Acid Jesus. He notes that some DJs choose names suggestive of their roles 'as powerful actors who lead their public into ecstatic states, e.g., Hypnotist, Grroverider, Shamen' (22). The DJs whom Androutsopoulos names are all men.

The common practice of adopting a stage name and Androutsopoulos' research on naming raise the question of the significance of naming practices among female DJs and producers. Of the producers, DJs and MCs[5] I interviewed, approximately half had adopted stage names at some point in their careers. Contrary to my initial sense that there might be something noteworthy about gender and naming, the decision about whether to adopt a stage name appears to be highly individual and in cases where women chose to do so, their choices did not follow any specific power or gender trends. The following passages from interviews with women who adopted stage names reflect this conclusion.

Sarah FAB [Sarah Pascoe] explains:

Sarah FAB comes from Forever and Beyond, which was our company, and we shortened it to FAB. I sent out our emails like that and people knew me as that. It's a stage name, like a band calling itself Aerosmith. I always go with the FAB name ... I like to be able to use my name but have enough of something different than my [birth] name. Just because me personally I find it weird to have someone come up and call me by a different name so it was like I wanted to have something with it but I didn't want it to just be Sarah, but I wouldn't want it to be something totally different like Psycho Bitch.

(5 December 2004 interview)

Polywog [Rebecca Corbett] explains the process of choosing her DJ name:

I got the name because I didn't want to be DJ Rebecca and there is one now but I also wanted a separate identity. I invented that spelling myself because I looked it up. I was doing a mix in 1990 or '91 and I was just going like, 'Fuck, I'm just a polywog' and I was like, 'Oh,' and it just stuck.

(16 May 2005 interview)

Sarah Randolph has two names, one of which she reserves specifically for her electro glam/ghetto tech persona:

My friend came up with the name: 'We should call you Seraphim.' It means angels of the highest order because I used to have a thing about angels, or my guardian angels, and sometimes I've felt like I've been other people's guardian angel, so to me that was pretty cool. Delush came from when I was getting kind of known for drum and bass stuff with Seraphim, so Sarah Delush was my ghetto tech other kind of music name.

(6 May 2005 interview)

Explaining the construction of her DJ name Queen Agnes B [Agnes Borysewicz] said:

You know I was kinda going by Agnes B for a while when I first started. Then this promoter was telling me, 'Oh, you know, you should add a little something to it.' I was like, 'What do you mean?' [He was] like, Miss Agnes B, Lady, something, whatever.' I was like, 'Queen Agnes B?' He was like, 'Oh yes.' My logo is the bee thing; the stinger on the bee is actually a [record] needle.

(13 May 2005 interview)

From 2000 to 2003 Layla Dudley DJ'd under the name Velo, then changed her name in 2003. '[My dad] got me riding bicycles. My first DJ name was Velo, the French word for bicycle.' After feeling burned out on DJing she retreated for awhile, then decided to resurface with a more laid-back attitude. 'I managed to get the domain name djlayla.com and it was available, wow that's a sign. That's what I want to be known as, Layla or just DJ Layla. I don't feel the need to be strict, hardcore, or official about it anymore' (13 July 2005 interview).

As these quotes reflect, choosing a name is an idiosyncratic process for women in EDM that, like the naming of rock bands, does not necessarily follow any common patterns. Even women who chose not to adopt a stage name did so for different reasons. Some based their decision on viewing their stage performance as an extension of their life offstage. Melissa Sautter explains her decision to drop the 'a' from her name and substitute a 'y' for the 'i'. 'I have to say that anytime somebody calls me Melyss I'm so psyched with my DJ name, cause I don't think I'd be able to learn to respond to DJ Butterflywings, DJ Glowstick, [or] DJ Puffy Backpack' (16 May 2005 interview). Others, like Melissa [Melissa Burnell], simply have no desire for an alternate name: 'I'm not much of a nickname person. Nothing ever stuck. I don't think that fits me and a lot of my friends have DJ names I don't like and I just think that they're cheesy' (19 May 2005 interview).

One noteworthy element of women DJs' names is the number of women who choose to use only their first name as their DJ name. While this was not an issue when there were so few women DJs, by the mid-2000s it was becoming a problem because too many women have the same name and identification of DJs has become confusing. In the future, more women are likely to either adopt stage names or use their first and last names to promote their EDM activities, if for no other reason than to minimize confusion. This is especially important for women who want to expand their recognition beyond their local communities.

Conclusion

In the context of EDM's emergence in the post-feminist age of the 2000s, women in EDM want and expect the freedom to represent themselves however they choose. After all, as DJs they have already defied the gendered expectations for women in EDM, which have traditionally confined them to the dance floor or to non-music related service work such as bartending or PR. Yet while they have made noteworthy inroads, there is still some distance to travel. Despite women DJs' assertions that they are fully in control of their stage personas, the range of DJ identities available to them remains limited, shaped by external forces both within and beyond EDM culture.

The sex kitten image is the DJ identity embodied by most superstar female DJs, yet most of the women I interviewed were fervently opposed to this persona. This image reflects third-wave feminist sensibilities that promote 'embracing girlieness as well as power' (Baumgardner and Richards, cited in Harris 2004: 59), where 'girlieness' references a style of femininity comprising sexy clothes, hair and make-up. In her critique of this definition of the 'third-wave', McRobbie (2009) astutely argues that 'this is a polemic about affirmation, that young women have more or less gained all the freedom they need' (158). In other words, while the sex kitten image may signify to some degree women's power and control over their representations, it also signifies the limits of women's power both within and beyond EDM culture. The fact that so many superstar female DJs embody this persona speaks to the ongoing objectification of women in EDM's male-centric spaces.

Rejecting the objectification they believe the sex kitten persona invites from men and the judgement it elicits from other female DJs, t-shirt DJs opt for the more 'natural' attire of jeans and t-shirts, which is what male DJs usually wear. In this case, the mirroring of a style typical of their male counterparts also suggests the limited choices available to them. This is not an environment in which anything goes; on the contrary, firm boundaries still circumscribe their style options.

The third category, dyke DJs, applies to gay DJs who either embody visible dyke identities via particular hair styles or clothing or choose to self-identify as dykes for social and/ or political reasons regardless of their appearance. Gay women who embody a visible dyke identity receive more support from male DJs because men are unlikely to see their sexuality as providing them with a competitive edge the way they may think it does for most heterosexual women or any women – gay or straight – who embody the sex kitten persona. Notably, dyke DJs remain bound by the routine practices of EDM culture in the sense that at times they are still represented as objects. However, unlike heterosexual female DJs they also take on the role of objectifier, as in the case of the DJ Irene album cover discussed above.

Overall, perhaps the most problematic aspect of women DJs' identities is the need to constantly monitor the extent to which their sexuality influences their image. Consistently, the most successful women – as measured by factors such as paid bookings (especially beyond their local community), the release of DJ mixes and other income generators that enable them to earn a living from DJing – are heterosexual women who either willingly embrace the sex kitten persona or, in the case of dyke DJs such as DJ Irene, embody the roles of both the objectified and the objectifier.

The following chapter raises the discussion of individual identity formation to the collective level. It seeks to piece together and examine the alternative discourses women in EDM create, both online and offline, that privilege collaboration over competition. In particular, it outlines the significance of women-centred geographical and Internet spaces such as potlucks, listservs and e-zines.

Notes

1. Despite the apolitical nature of much rap music and hip hop culture today, Cheryl Keyes (2002) argues that the image of black women rappers is political in nature because "'it calls attention to aspects of women's bodies that are considered undesirable by mainstream American standards of beauty,'" such as full breasts, rounded buttocks and ample thighs. She goes on to illustrate the ways in which

    > black women rappers use their performances as platforms to refute, deconstruct, and reconstruct alternative visions of their identity—vehicles by which they seek empowerment, make choices, and create spaces for themselves and other sistas.

    (p. 209)

    Increasingly, female hip hop artists are making social justice issues and political activism their central mission. Detroit-based Invincible's work in particular addresses issues such as mental health and the Israeli – Palestinian conflict.
2. In 2000, scholar and electronic musician Tara Rodgers established Pinknoises.com to 'make resources on production methods more accessible to women and girls, and to provide an online space where issues of music and gender could be discussed' (Rodgers 2010: p. 3). The project has since migrated to Facebook, where it maintains an active conversation.
3. 'Rock Star Shots' is the name of the company hired for the photo shoot.
4. Psychedelic-trance, otherwise known as 'psy-trance', is an EDM subgenre that has a faster beat (generally from 125 to 150 beats per minute) than many other forms of EDM. It features prominent bass beats and varying rhythms and melodies.
5. The role of the MC is to provide vocals in the form of singing, rapping or talking over the DJ's set to hype up the crowd.

Chapter 3

Potlucks, Listservs and E-Zines: Networking and
Social Capital in Action

W omen in EDM have invested considerable time and effort in forming connections with other female DJs in their own cities, across the United States and internationally in an effort to overcome the sexism and marginalization they experience in EDM culture. Since the 1990s, many have endeavoured to create a dialogue among women to foster social and professional support.

In one of our first conversations, I asked Forest Green [Melissa Green] why she dedicates so much time and energy to networking with other women DJs. She responded enthusiastically:

Oh man, the support. The support of other women who understand truly what it's like is one of the biggest reasons, I think. All the sharing you can do with one another from our own experiences. Also, just the sliminess that occurs in the entertainment industry. [You can] save your friends – all the sisters everywhere – a lot of trouble just by [saying], 'Hey, that guy is a total slime ball, and this happened,' though it's not necessarily a guy. There are certainly slimy women too. The power that you have as a group as opposed to an individual. It's harder to pull something over on a group. The friendship. I don't know, so many things, really.

(Forest Green, 9 May 2005 interview)

This emphasis on the importance of dialogue among women in EDM and the power that can be gained from this kind of community building became increasingly apparent with each conversation I had with these women.

Locally, women have established DJ collectives that have both face-to-face and online components. Most, though not all, of the women interviewed were early technology and Internet adopters. They were quick to create a strong Internet presence that encouraged communication among female DJs in local and distant locations. The listservs and websites that offered some of the first networking opportunities have been influential for women not only in the United States, but internationally as well. As this research shows, personal DJ websites are also a key component in extending one's network.

In essence, most women DJs – regardless of the DJ image or stage persona they adopt – would prefer it if their sex did not impact the way they are judged as DJs. Building on Chapter 2's discussion of image, this chapter explores some of the most prominent geographical and Internet-based networks for women in EDM since the 1990s. I argue that such spaces are distinctive and vital to women and their ability to overcome their marginalization in EDM culture. Created by and for women, these networks provide social and emotional support and, via their networking capabilities, help women build much-needed subcultural and social capital. As I discuss in more detail below, the accumulation of such capital is empowering. Access to 'insider' knowledge and important individuals – such as club management, promoters, booking agents and other DJs – is vital to advancing one's DJ skills and visibility. In turn, the expectation is that as female DJs and producers become more commonplace, they will have fewer issues to deal with related to their sexuality.

In line with much of the analysis in this book, the case studies and examples examined here complicate the significance of feminism for the women participating in these networking practices. The networking actions of women in EDM have much in common with those of the Riot Grrrls in the 1990s, whose identification with feminism was central to their mission of female empowerment and positive identity construction. Yet, as I explain in Chapter 2, even though they share some commonalities with feminist activists such as the Riot Grrrls, many women in EDM do not label themselves or their actions as feminist. In fact, as Chapter 4 illustrates more explicitly, it is more common for female DJs to reject this label, despite their efforts to organize women for the purpose of overcoming their unequal representation and treatment in EDM culture. In addition to the contemporary post-feminist climate that has encouraged women to reject a feminist label, female DJs may also be reluctant to label themselves as feminist, despite their feminist actions, because they operate in a club culture environment where men hold most of the power. To do so could create more distance between them and men in these spaces.

To be clear, I am not imposing a feminist label on women EDM DJs. Instead, I am viewing their discursive and material efforts at community building and networking through a feminist lens. In my use of the label 'feminist' I am less concerned with the specific fissures between feminist waves – notably between second wave feminism and the third wave that began in the 1990s – and more interested in the threads that connect contemporary women's issues with those of the past. In other words, even though numerous descriptions (Roiphe 1993; Walker 2001) have characterized the relationship between second and third wave feminism as confrontational and uncooperative, if not hostile, there is much to be gained from emphasizing the continuity between waves and generations. As Tara Rodgers astutely notes in the introduction to her book *Pink Noises*:

Typical 'wave' models of feminism, which describe feminist movements as succeeding each other temporally in a linear historical progression, and tend to posit strictly defined generations of women as irrevocably at odds with each other's interests, are inadequate representations of women's complex identifications.

(18)

In recognition and support of this continuity, I use the term 'feminist' without reference to waves to describe specific practices of women in EDM, such as their consciousness-raising efforts to identify and address structural inequalities discussed below.

From here I introduce the concepts of social and subcultural capital before moving on to offer a firsthand look at monthly potluck meetings in Portland, Oregon and their connection to the Internet. Next, I turn my analysis to the Sisterdjs listerv and the importance of personal websites. The chapter ends with an examination of *Shejay*, the most comprehensive e-zine dedicated to women in EDM.

Social and subcultural capital

To be successful, DJs must have access to not only the technical and musical knowledge central to DJ and EDM culture but also to the key players in these scenes such as promoters, club management and other DJs. Thus it is vital for women to have access to the spaces and conversations in which important information and individuals circulate. The women interviewed for this project possess varying degrees of both of these forms of capital. By subcultural capital I am invoking Sarah Thornton's (1996) conception of the term that builds on Pierre Bourdieu's writings on the links between taste and social structure. Bourdieu's theoretical framework for understanding these connections includes discussion of cultural, economic and social capital. Thornton describes social capital as stemming 'not so much from *what* you know as *who* you know (and who knows you)' (10) and subcultural capital as the rules that govern a particular subculture. She further explains that subcultural capital can be objectified in the form of fashionable haircuts and well-assembled record collections or embodied in the form of being 'in the know' or using (but not over-using) current slang. Hence social capital is one component or form of subcultural capital. What the women I interviewed share is the desire to increase their subcultural capital with regards to EDM. Even for those who are well connected within women-centred EDM spaces, there is room for growth, particularly in moving beyond these networks and extending their presence to the diverse, global nodes of EDM culture. Such a move would increase their bridging social capital – the heterogeneous set of 'weak' ties in a social network, which refer to the loose connections between people that enable information diffusion across networks (Ellison, Lampe, Steinfield and Vitak 2010). Expanding one's social network is desirable and useful because it creates more opportunities for getting to know the right people as well as for acquiring pertinent information. Though less vital, female DJs also benefit from forming close-knit connections – what are called 'strong' ties – with other women and men in EDM culture because these connections indicate close bonding relationships that provide emotional and personal support.

In his acclaimed book *Bowling Alone* (2000) Robert Putnam discusses the relationship between community and social capital, which he defines as 'the connections among individuals – social networks and the norms of reciprocity and trustworthiness that arise from them' (19). Comparing this description to 'civic virtue' he goes on to say that, the difference here is that 'social capital' calls attention to the fact that civic virtue is more powerful when embedded in a dense network of reciprocal social relations. A society of many virtuous but isolated individuals is not necessarily rich in social capital.

(19)

In other words, numerous individuals need to regularly communicate with one another in order for them to collectively tap into and benefit from each other's knowledge and practices. Putnam makes a point to stress that social capital involves more than 'individual clout and companionship' in the sense that it can have 'externalities' that affect the wider community in ways that are by no means always positive. For instance, '[s]ocial inequalities may be embedded in social capital. Norms and networks that serve some groups may obstruct others, particularly if the norms are discriminatory or the networks socially segregated' (358). These examples speak to women's experiences in EDM and DJ culture in the sense that the norms and networks that govern these cultures and from which men have benefitted are the same practices that at times are responsible for the marginalization of women's participation. The positive effects that female DJs and producers can incur from increasing their social and subcultural capital – in terms of an increase in technical and musical knowledge and access to key players – can lead to more gigs and in turn more recognition, which is likely to result in more money. In turn, an increase in economic capital can further expand women's possibilities and contributions to EDM culture. For example, some women cite a lack of financial resources as a major reason why they do not produce music despite their interest in doing so, a point on which I elaborate in Chapter 5.

Overall, Putnam views the build up of social capital as not only positive but essential to restoring American community for the twenty-first century that he argues declined significantly in the latter half of the twentieth century. Specifically, he points to a handful of counter-trends, including participation in self-help and support groups and, most notably, changes in telecommunications as important contributors to a potential renewal. Writing in the 1990s, Putnam was cautionary about what could be said about the connection between social capital and Internet technology. Yet he predicted, based on the history of the telephone and on the early Internet use, that online communication 'w[ould] turn out to *complement*, not *replace*, face-to-face communities' (179, italics in original). Research on social network sites in the 2000s (Ellison, Steinfield and Lampe 2007; Boyd 2008) concluded similar findings.

To some extent, the efforts of women in EDM to build community and increase social capital also support Putnam's forecast. In particular, the monthly Portland potluck I visited involves women getting together face-to-face, yet its coordination also relies on computer-mediated communication. Other examples I discuss, such as the Sisterdjs mailing list and the e-zine *Shejay*, exist solely as online spaces that provide women with opportunities to build social capital through networking.

One of the most influential women-centred DJ collectives that emerged in the 1990s was the Sister collective. It began in San Francisco in 1997 as Sister SF and eventually expanded to other US cities, most successfully in New York City (Sister NYC) and Portland, Oregon

(Sister PDX). The detailed history, influence and Internet presence of the collective is the subject of Chapter 4. I turn now to a discussion of the monthly potlucks hosted by Layla [Layla Dudley], DJ and founding member of Sister PDX, in Portland, Oregon.

Portland potluck

An exciting example of a local community-building effort among female DJs is a series of monthly potlucks in Portland, Oregon that ran for several years in the early 2000s. I was fortunate enough to attend one of these meetings on a warm Sunday afternoon in July 2003. Since 2001, Layla had been hosting potlucks on the second Sunday of every month. Almost none of the women knew each other before Layla set up the Sister PDX mailing list and began advertising the potlucks. She was motivated to start the gatherings after meeting with members of the Sister SF collective, who were in town playing at a local coffee shop. She initially read a post they sent to the Sisterdjs mailing list (discussed further below) asking if anyone could get them any gigs. She explains the evolution as follows:

> At the time I knew this guy who was starting this techno coffee shop thing. I was like, 'Hey, I bet I can get them a gig'. I went ahead and asked this guy and we made it a free night. They were totally down. They wanted the exposure and we promoted it and got a nice crowd of people out to hear break and jungle[1] and it was a good time. I sat down and got to talking with them in 2001, so two years ago, and was inspired by them.
>
> (13 July 2003 interview)

Layla called her gathering Sister PDX.[2] She sometimes made flyers advertising the potluck to hand out to women she knew and women who came up to her after gigs. She also posted information on the Sisterdjs mailing list. Sister PDX and the collective's monthly potlucks highlight the intricate online and offline networking that led to the monthly potlucks and their role in providing a safe and supportive space for women.

I arrived at Layla's converted loft apartment just after 3:30 pm, and for the next four hours I casually observed the event and asked questions. A relaxed yet well organized meeting took place from 4 to 5 pm. Layla and three other members of the Sister PDX Internet mailing list gathered on the couch and the floor to talk about the future of both the potluck and the mailing list in light of Layla's impending move to Eugene, Oregon to study dance at the University of Oregon. Layla talked about passing on her responsibilities as handing over the role of 'whip cracker'. While no one offered to take over all of her responsibilities, a decision was made to continue both the listserv and the monthly gathering, with the women taking turns hosting the potluck at their homes.

The group also discussed upcoming gigs they were in the process of organizing and promoting at local clubs and coffee shops. A few mentioned that they were volunteering at Portland's upcoming Rock 'n' Roll Camp for Girls. It is significant that the Portland camp was the first of its kind in the United States, and its success has led to the creation of similar camps across the country. Also, in the 1990s Riot Grrrls' organized feminist punk events in a fashion similar to those discussed at the potluck, using DIY techniques and strategies. The hub of the Riot Grrrl movement was Olympia, Washington, located just a few hours north of Portland. The proximity of these two cities shows the support that DIY women's music efforts have received in the Northwest.

Just after 5 pm, six more women arrived. Some were carrying trays of food, others crates of records. Most of the women present were in their 20s but their DJ knowledge and experience covered a wide range, from those who had been DJing for years to a few women who had been DJing for fewer than three months. Gradually the women moved to the other half of the room, where Layla kept her turntables and records. Conveniently, the next room over was the kitchen. The women wandered back and forth from the kitchen to the turntable area. One woman cooked corn on the cob while another set up a fruit tray that included fresh grapes and strawberries. Layla apologized for not preparing her usual batch of hummus because she had been out of town until just before the meeting.

For the next two hours the women ate, played records and asked each other questions about music, local promoters and DJ techniques. Layla stood by the turntables most of the time and encouraged the most inexperienced women to practice spinning records while she acted as a guide. After a few hours, the crowd slowly began to disperse until Layla and I were the only two people left in the apartment. As they left, the women assured one another that they would reconvene in a month's time, if not sooner, for another potluck.

Figure 3.1: Researcher with DJs at Portland potluck (2003).

Figure 3.2: Layla instructs a beginner DJ (2003).

When asked about the purpose of the monthly potlucks, Layla characterized them as 'a friendly place for women to discuss DJ practices'. She commented on the evolution of the potlucks over the course of several years, noting:

It's up and down. Some days, it's so random. Some days two or three people will come. We'll kick it. [I'll] show you how to do this, show you what I do. Other days we got some publicity for it in free [local] papers. I had people emailing me saying, 'Oh my God, this is awesome'. In January 2003, February and March it blew up for a few months there. I moved to this space, then it shrank. A lot of the same people come and I always end up getting one or two new people. Sometimes I'll get almost all new people. People hear about it through the grapevine.

(Layla, 13 July 2003 interview)

When asked about her motivation for organizing and hosting the potlucks, Layla thought about the question for a moment before answering:

I have a lot of that teacher in me. If I can show somebody how to start it won't be that intimidating to them. They won't have to try to learn from their guy friends. I just thought it'd be a fun thing to do … I think in some ways I have been that role [model] or that seed here in the Portland scene to some of those women at least because I was so willing to step out and say come over and hang out with me. We'll do this, we'll have a good time, we'll get together and we'll be a girls club. It'll be fun.

Through these informal exchanges Layla served as a mentor for other local women interested in pursuing DJing. Accordingly, women used both the private space of the potlucks and their public DJ activity in coffee shops and clubs to strengthen their social and subcultural capital related to DJ and EDM culture. In the private space of the potluck they shared information and taught each other DJ skills that then enabled them to play out in public, where they had opportunities to socialize with other local men and women involved with EDM. By late 2002 these gatherings, which continued through 2005, led to an official invitation from Sister SF to create a Portland branch of the women-centred DJ collective. The far-reaching impact and accomplishments of Sister SF and its progeny in Portland (Sister PDX) and New York City (Sister NYC) are the subjects of Chapter 4. Next, I turn to a more detailed examination of the purpose and function of the Sisterdjs listserv where Layla first came into contact with members of Sister SF.

Sisterdjs

Group communication on the Internet was not a new phenomenon at the time I conducted the fieldwork for this project. Early on in the life of the Internet, people gravitated to the possibility of forming new connections with others who shared their interests. In the late 1970s the first-ever mailing list was created. It was called SF-lovers and was a space for fans to come together to discuss their love of science fiction (Rheingold 1994).

Since then an unimaginable number of lists and discussion forums have been established, focusing on nearly every conceivable interest, hobby and concern. The positive experiences of participants have led to the characterization of many of these spaces as virtual communities, a phenomenon that scholars have been studying for decades. While the precise definition of such spaces remains in flux, all emphasize to varying extents the personal connections and meaningful new social formations created online (Baym 1999, 2010; Jenkins 2006; Rheingold 1994).

More recently, scholars have taken an interest in the role of online communication in fostering social capital. In surveys of undergraduate students about their use of the social networking site Facebook, Ellison, Steinfield and Lampe (2007) found that while young people use Facebook primarily to keep in contact with people they know offline, the site helped students both maintain and create more bridging social capital because participation does not require a lot of time or work. Analysis of threads from the Sisterdjs mailing list demonstrates the ways in which the list exemplified online community in the sense that meaningful personal communication was exchanged and new social formations were created in this virtual space. Moreover, these exchanges increased the social and subcultural capital of its participants.

Dozens of mailing lists about EDM culture were created in the 1990s. The website hyperreal. org continues to archive discussions from listservs that were organized geographically in the United States so that individuals could be 'in the know' about events happening in close physical proximity to them. There are numerous reasons why many of the lists are no longer active. Their activity level peaked in the late 1990s at the height of rave culture's popularity, and similar to other lists, today most of them have been replaced by Google calendars or pages and groups on social networking sites.

In 1996, at the height of the listserv activity, the influential listserv Sisterdjs was created. Through this mailing list many women, including many of the DJs in Portland affiliated with Sister PDX, were exposed to and became part of a network of female DJs for the first time. It was via the Sisterdjs list that I initially communicated with many of the women I later interviewed for this project. Because the list served as my initial point of contact with many study participants, I include here some of the discursive exchanges that took place on the list prior to my fieldwork. These discussions show not only the importance of the list to its participants because it provided them with an instant female DJ community that was otherwise lacking but also, and perhaps more importantly, the symbiotic relationship between women-centred EDM communities on the Internet and their interaction offline.

Despite the fact that the data examined here precede the explosion of social networking and music sites such as Last.fm, the online activities of these women DJs demonstrate what Baym has since (2007) described as 'networked collectivism'. Similar to the Swedish indie music fans in her study, these women also were part of various loose collectives of associated individuals that together bound networks. According to Baym, 'this sort of social formation poses the methodological challenge of how to bound the object of study'. Yet such work is important because so few studies 'explore the connections amongst these disparate online platforms, despite the fact that people's online activities are almost always distributed across multiple sites'. There are many more online platforms today than a decade ago, yet the connections discussed here reveal not only the early stages of networked collectivism online, but also the ways in which such online practices integrate with and extend participants' lives beyond the Internet. After all, women DJs participate in these online spaces to enhance their DJing experiences offline.

It is important to keep in mind that cities like Portland, San Francisco and New York, which all had chapters of Sister at the time of my fieldwork, represent rare exceptions in that a significant number of women participate in local EDM scenes. San Francisco in particular continues to be one of the most supportive and largest communities for women DJs not only in the United States but also globally. As XJS [Annie Shaw] recounted to me in 2003:

In the past seven years I've been spinning nothing has changed. I've played in Prague and Barcelona and London. I've played around the world a bunch of places. I've been told I couldn't get into the DJ booth because I was a girl. I couldn't be the DJ. [That was] five years ago in Munich. [I said] I'm the DJ [and was told] no you're not. Munich is not a particularly backward city.

(XJS, 22 July 2003 interview)

As XJS's experiences demonstrate, as recently as the early 2000s the presence of a woman behind the turntables was a rare site. Even today women DJs continue to be the exception rather than the rule. Because there have historically been so few female DJs, they have been more likely to network with one another in online settings such as the Sisterdjs mailing list as opposed to first meeting offline.

Although she is a San Francisco resident, Forest Green still spoke enthusiastically about the Internet's invaluable networking opportunities for women. In her words:

The other thing that's been really cool about the online, it's been able to bring women from all over the US and the world together to start networking as women, not an against-the-men thing, just that there are a lot of things that are unique to women and us in this industry. There is a boys club ... once you start getting up into things that are actually going to pay you any money, or at least something that could truly be a career, there is competition. Obviously lots of people want to do it. So women helping each other, working as teams, and also getting past all the BS and the media, [and how we're] socialized not to work as teams. The sooner all of us get past that and work together and network the more we're all going to benefit in the end.

(personal communication, 7 July 2003)

In an effort to encourage dialogue between women DJs, DJ Dazy set up Sisterdjs in 1996. Although she is a Salt Lake City, Utah native, she was living in Portland, Oregon at the time. She relocated to San Jose, California in 1997 before finally settling in Los Angeles in 1998. DJ Dazy was an active DJ until the birth of her daughter in 2004. From 1996 to 2004, visitors to the Sisterdjs website were greeted with this statement:

In 1996 I created this list as a resource for women djs across the world. We (women djs) are still the minority in the large male dominated scene. I feel that creating a safe place to ask questions about djing will help the growth of women djs out in the world.

This list is mainly a support group for new and experienced women to exchange information about anything DJ related.

(DJ Dazy, http://www.sisterdjs.com)

The list was one of the earliest women-centred EDM spaces online. By 2000, it had over 300 members and included women from Europe, Japan and Australia (Soapbox girls: 2000). In 2001, 67 women had bios on the site. As a participant-observer on the list from

2001 to 2004 – primarily as a lurker – I observed the numerous and varied EDM- and DJ-related issues women discussed on the list.

In the fall of 2001 I coded three months' worth of posts using 29 themes, several of which reflected one of Baym's (2010) primary qualities of virtual community, 'shared resources and support'. Some of the categories into which these themes were coded include: 'giving DJing advice', 'helpful personal experience stories', 'beat matching', 'bf[boyfriend]/gf [girlfriend] hates the music/turn that down', 'gear concerns/questions', 'I can relate' and 'record care'. Posts from threads with subject headings such as 'pigeon holed', 'record care' and 'boyfriend hates the music' demonstrate the extraordinary level of detail and personal experience women DJs are willing to disclose for not only their own but also each other's benefit. The personal experiences and information shared in these threads increased the bridging social capital of participants, and may have augmented their bonding social capital as well. Their bridging social capital was increased because the very act of exchanging information raises their subcultural capital on two levels. It makes them privy to 'insider' information and gives them access to other female DJs, which expands the size of their DJ networks. Also, while there is no direct evidence that these interactions led to increases in bonding social capital, it is possible that the disclosure of personal information on threads like 'boyfriends hates the music' led to DJs developing close-knit connections off the listserv's public space.

The uniqueness and value of the open communication on Sisterdjs becomes more apparent when contrasted with a non-gender specific music-focused mailing list like Rocklist, which was dedicated to the academic discussion of popular music. Popular music scholar Norma Coates (1998) explains that she joined the list in the hope that it 'would provide me with an opportunity to discuss my ideas, especially those about rock and gender formed by my experience of loving rock but not recognizing "myself" in it' (78). Coates' expectation that she would have a voice in this space coincides with early hypotheses about communication in cyberspace, which predicted that reduced social cues would lead to a redistribution of social power online because factors such as race and gender would become irrelevant (Walther 1992). Yet, despite these early predictions Coates and other women encountered 'the same old scene. My messages and those from other women, particularly when we tried to discuss gender and rock, were ignored, argued with, or trivialized. A male respondent would generally proffer the "correct" take on an issue' (78).

Coates' experience on Rocklist supports two claims about communication in cyberspace. First, it upholds the observation that 'most arguments for the democratic potential of cyberspace are based on a naive dismissal of the relations of power that construct and permit social interaction' (Travers 2003: 223). Second, it supports Gurak's (2001) findings that men dominate Internet-based conversations in terms of both the volume of participation and agenda setting, even on feminist topics (cited in Travers 2003). Thus, there continues to be a need for women-centred spaces both offline and online. For the women on Rocklist, this meant taking their discussion of gender and rock elsewhere, with the formation of their own group they called 'Clitlist'.

The range of topics covered and the level of detail divulged on Sisterdjs indicate the significant extent to which women felt comfortable asking questions and disclosing personal information for the purpose of assisting and supporting one another. Dialogue on the list also reflected several 'communicative virtues' that help initiate and sustain dialogue over time (Burbules and Rice 1991).

> These virtues include tolerance, patience, respect for differences, a willingness to listen, the inclination to admit that one may be mistaken, the ability to reinterpret or translate one's own concerns in a way that makes them comprehensible to others, the self-imposition of restraint in order that others may 'have a turn' to speak, and the disposition to express one's self honestly and sincerely.
>
> (cited in Travers 2003: 231)

A thread titled 'boyfriend hates the music???????' brought to the foreground the issue of unsupportive romantic partners. The initial post began with the following statement:

> 'turn that down!!' is a frequently heard phrase in my household. The fact that he hates the music doesn't bother me, I couldn't care less but, what bothers me is that he doesn't ever want me to get out there and spin in clubs or at parties, he is an old school jaded ex-raver and I guess he had some bad experiences, but he is very angry towards the whole scene for some reason. this comes down on me because, i love the music, in fact im obsessed with it! [sic]

Another subscriber, Marisha, draws on her past and present experiences with boyfriends to offer some advice.

> While i am used to most people thinking me and my music are weird ... it did kind of suck that my bf did not take an interest in something that is important to me. He wouldn't have to like it or be expected to be my drooling groupie at every show ... all I wanted was that he gave it a chance and made an effort to show support once in a while. I also wanted him to understand once in a while when I couldn't hang out with him because i had a gig, and not get upset. Needless to say i am not with him anymore. [sic]

In contrast, her current boyfriend

> is NOT 'in the scene' so there is no jealousy or competitiveness or other bullshit that comes with that ... no bringing politics and alliances and all that nonsense into things. That is also why I would not date another DJ ... especially not a jungle dj because this city's too small for that. I've lost male friends who have been threatened by me as a DJ so I don't even wanna get started on a BF! (hey props to those out there who are dating fellow djs, happily with no problems!)
>
> *<advice section of this email here>**

I would definitely probe more deeply into this double standard that's going on: he has a problem with YOU DJing but not his friends ... there is more to that then [sic] just 'bitterness at the scene'.

These posts illustrate the difficulties women in EDM may face when it comes to maintaining romantic relationships. Although the examples I draw on are from heterosexual relationships, the fact that spending time on DJ-related activities takes time away from significant others is equally true for women in gay relationships. The public disclosure of these experiences on the list generated a lively thread in which several women shared personal relationship experiences, assessed the pros and cons of staying in relationships with unsupportive partners and discussed the potential signs of relationship abuse. It is reasonable to assume that these types of conversations are unique to women-centred spaces, especially given the sensitive subject matter and Travers's (2003) findings that when men are present they tend to dominate listserv participation. Additionally, the reference to the jungle subgenre in one of the posts speaks to the tight networks that can develop around a specific EDM subgenre in a local community. For women who feel excluded from these geographically bound, tightly knit communities, virtual spaces like Sisterdjs may be the only place they can turn to for support.

The thread labeled 'record care' exemplifies the way in which women-centred EDM spaces help women build subcultural capital. It also shows the altruism at work on the list despite the competitiveness that often plagues DJ culture. The initial post explained:

So this guy spilled beer on my record. It is my breakbeat remix of the Smurfs song and I have emotional attachment!!! Grrrrr! I dashed off to the record store to buy some of that record cleaning stuff. Friendly DJ store guy said not to buy it because it will leave a film on your records. He said he cleans his records with water and some rubbing alcohol and a soft cloth. I tried that but you can still hear that there is goo on the record!
My question to you wonderful ladies is how can I get this crap off!? How much rubbing alcohol to how much water (I know, should have asked at the store ...) What would happen if I tried with just alcohol?
Thanks so much as usual! loves [sic], ekb*

Below are a few excerpts from replies to ekb*'s initial post.

When it comes to my tunes i am a bit of a clean-o-maniac. What is the best way to clean and extend the life of vinyl. Esp. considering exposure to harsh environments like smoke, fingerprint grease, heat and other (avoidable or unavoidable) accidents. I've been told that Windex (window/glass) cleaning fluid is just as good (and the same thing) as the ten-dollar bottles of vinyl cleaning fluid. Is this true? For some inexplicable reason … my record shop has record cleaning fluid with no labels on the bottles plus i dont have a chemist friend to run some comparison tests (!). (sic)

Much love – Shara.

Hi all,

I've never had beer spilled on a record, but I have had dogs piss on them (yuck!) and to get it off, plain old water worked great. I would recommend just rinsing it off, don't rub, and patting it dry. Good luck!

~astrid~

I suggest getting a couple of crap records from salvation army or the deep discount bin, and try out different cleaning solutions on them. That way you won't run the risk of damaging the record you love.

Leigh

The responses to ekb*'s query about record care demonstrate the willingness of list participants to share inside knowledge about how to clean records in the way of friendly advice. Again, the space to ask such questions is significant because ekb* did not feel comfortable asking the record store clerk for more information, even though she refers to him as 'friendly DJ store guy' in her post. Clearly, she felt more comfortable asking the women on the list for further details.

In summary, the conversations on the list reflect characteristics of Burbules and Rice's (1991) communication virtues. Participants' willingness to listen to one another and the openness and sincerity of their posts characterize them as a virtual community. When asked if she felt like part of a DJ community, San José resident DJ Ara's [Heather Reagan] response supported this notion. 'I think online definitely. Because I don't play out much I don't feel part of South Bay's electronic music scene. Being there [online] and being aware and participating in discussions and learning, you learn so much' (DJ Ara, 20 June 2003 interview).

Not only were personal relationships created in cyberspace, but in many cases they also moved from the Internet to life offline. Forming connections that go beyond the Internet is especially significant for DJs because DJing is about performing for an audience. Thus the social and subcultural capital garnered online become much more useful when they translate to capital offline.

Iowa City outliers

The benefits gained from the acquisition of social and subcultural capital at the local level cannot be overestimated. The value of women-centred, geographically based spaces becomes even more apparent when speaking with women who live in a geographical context that provides little local support. From 2000 to 2005 there were only two known women DJs in Iowa City, Iowa, a university town in the Midwest. In the four years that I was an Iowa City resident (2000–2004) I had many conversations with DJ Miche [Michelle Higley] and Lady Espina [Natalia Espina] about the local EDM scene. At the time that 'scene' consisted of one record store, whose EDM section was run exclusively by men, and one venue that regularly supported EDM events.

According to DJ Miche, in the 18 years she had lived in Iowa City there had been only one other female DJ in the city (who had since moved to Detroit) besides herself and Lady Espina. She believed that one reason there were so few women DJs in Iowa City was that the male DJs in town were not especially welcoming of women's interest and efforts. As she explained,

> It depends on where you are and how you get treated. As a local DJ around here I get more respect when I'm out of town than when I'm here. If you can be a DJ in Iowa City you can be a DJ anywhere.
>
> (DJ Miche, 15 September 2003 interview)

In other words, if a woman's motivation to DJ does not falter in a town like Iowa City, then most likely she would succeed elsewhere, in communities that presumably offer more encouragement and assistance.

Because there were only two women DJs in town, there was no opportunity at this time to form a women-centred collective in Iowa City similar to those in San Francisco and Portland. It was also difficult to organize women-centred DJ events in an effort to promote female DJs, which as several women noted in their interviews, can encourage more women to take an interest in DJing. Thus, the only option for DJ Miche and Lady Espina was to try to form ties with the local male DJs. An animated Lady Espina conveyed her exasperation with the situation:

> You have the kids who throw their parties. They book the same DJs who are all their friends. They have the same time slots and I run into situations where, OK, you have the nine o'clock time slot and it's like, 'Woohoo, that's gonna be great,' and it gets annoying. I'd rather just be home. I'd rather just be watching a movie.
>
> (Lady Espina, 12 September 2003 interview)

At the EDM events Lady Espina is describing, the purpose of the DJ who plays the nine o'clock time slot is essentially to warm up the night for the DJs scheduled to play at a later hour. It is undesirable for a few reasons. First, this slot is usually given to the most inexperienced or least popular DJs and second, there are very few people on the dance floor at this time. On occasion Lady Espina did manage to secure later time slots at some noteworthy local events, DJing right before prominent headliners such as Detroit's

Terrence Parker. But such opportunities were few and far between. Despite the liberal atmosphere for which Iowa City is known, both Lady Espina and DJ Miche found it difficult to acquire the bridging capital needed to break through the 'boys club' mentality of the local EDM scene.

Personal websites

In addition to emphasizing the value of interactive Internet spaces such as the Sisterdjs mailing list, women highlighted the importance of personal websites for networking and building social capital. In *Girls Make Media* (2006), feminist media scholar Mary Celeste Kearney illustrates how young women are developing advanced computing skills in web design and construction despite the significantly smaller number of women in the IT field in comparison to men. Most of the 12 18- to 29-year-olds Kearney interviewed reported having no formal web design training, instead they taught themselves how to code by viewing the source code of other websites. Many of the women I interviewed also learned their web design skills through means other than formal education.

The San Francisco Bay Area's prominence in technology research and development meant that many of the women I interviewed had access to peers who were working in web design. One of the founding members and designer of the Sister SF website, XJS [Annie Shaw], casually remarked that everyone in San Francisco is either a programmer or a DJ. XJS is one of several DJs I interviewed who is a professional web designer. The Bay Area's role in the Internet boom in the late 1990s made web design a particularly lucrative career path, which several women including XJS claim to have learned via 'osmosis' from watching significant others and friends do it for a living. Some women also enrolled in community college courses to further their skills.

DJs were particularly motivated to acquire these skills through the opportunities personal home pages generated for them at the time of my fieldwork, which predated the boom of social networking sites. Samira [Samira Vijghen] was a graduate student in English at the University of California, Berkeley when she became interested in web design for this reason. She recalled:

> I taught myself. I wanted a site when I started DJing. [I] had one of my friends do it and realized the value of websites if you keep the content current. People won't visit it if it's outdated. [I] started feeling bad asking my friend to update it. Next thing I know I started building everyone I know websites. Look at code all day long and so that's how I got started with web design. [I] would have never thought in a million years that I'd be hired as a web designer and here I am. I love doing it.
>
> (Samira, 20 May 2005 interview)

Samira's web design skills had an additional positive impact on her DJing.

[I] build sites for up-and-coming labels, which means that I can contribute to the producers that I really love and I really want to help them out and at the same time they're sending me all their promos months before they come out so it's a good deal.

(Samira, 20 May 2005 interview)

Because timeliness matters so much for DJs, the most beneficial part of this exchange for Samira is not that she gets records for free, but that she receives them long before they are available to other DJs. At the same time, being known by local producers and record labels helps her secure DJ gigs.

What began as unpaid labour led to Samira's decision to change her career path. Samira notes that in addition to her self-taught web design skills, having XJS as a reference helped her obtain full-time work building digital libraries for universities. She was thus able to translate the technical expertise gained from engagement with new media into a career opportunity.

Even DJs who do not earn an income from web design recognize the PR function of their websites and the need to develop the skills to keep them updated. According to DJ Denise [Denise Rees]:

A website is key to being a successful DJ, at least for people who are starting or people who are kind of already established and out there. I guess they don't necessarily need one but it wouldn't hurt them either. But for people who are just kind of getting started, how

Figure 3.3: Screenshot from DJ Denise's website, www.djdenise.com (2011).

else are you going to be able to spread the word about yourself? I've actually gotten a lot of my out-of-town bookings through my site, through people just doing a search, through other people's links [I] got random bookings. Last time I went to Hawaii was through a link or through my website so it's definitely good for letting people know out-of-state that you exist.

(DJ Denise, 8 July 2003 interview)

She explained her process of learning web design as follows:

My brother bought my domain name through his work. One of my friends taught me the basic HTML tags and whatever and then from there I just started using online tutorials and stuff. Last September I took a web design class and learned a bit more. This past semester I took a Flash class. It was not as difficult as I thought it would be.

(DJ Denise, 8 July 2003 interview)

In DJ Denise's case it was her relationship with her brother and a friend – people with whom she presumably had strong ties – that motivated her to build a website, which in turn created new possibilities for increasing her bridging capital.

The typical DJ website displays past gigs, a calendar of future bookings, MP3s of past DJ sets and some mix of diaries, pictures, links, guest books and discussion forums.[3] A website enables DJs to post information about their recent DJ activities, upcoming schedule and latest mixes. Discussion forums allow their users to read posts and engage in conversations, but they are primarily spaces for fan postings and rarely stimulate dialogue among DJs. Websites are also useful PR tools that help DJs establish legitimacy among booking agents, club owners and event coordinators. Nonetheless, a drawback to using individual web pages as a primary vehicle for publicity is their potential to be lost among the myriad websites in cyberspace. Overall, personal websites provide an additional medium through which DJs can network and promote themselves, thereby building social capital.

Shejay

Like personal websites, electronic magazines or 'e-zines' provide EDM artists with opportunities to network and increase their visibility, as well as to discursively intervene in EDM and DJ culture. These texts provide an effective means for women to publicize their work as DJs and producers while maintaining a DIY ethos. In her analysis of Riot Grrrls, Mavis Bayton (1998) traces the historical importance of fanzines to the movement. Bayton notes that the production and distribution of zines was essential to early punk culture in the late 1970s, then declined until the early 1990s. The zine format resurfaced among Riot

Grrrls, who used it to discuss a variety of feminist topics including sexism, discrimination, sexual abuse, body image and eating disorders, among others.

Similarly, e-zines like *Shejay* circulate alternative narratives of female DJs and producers that highlight their music and technology skills. These publications challenge the mass-mediated discourse that focuses on the images of female DJs more so than their musical pursuits. What is more, these mass-mediated representations tend to be either of female DJs who conform to narrow beauty standards, or else of models – most of whom are white-posing as DJs to sell consumer goods. As a DIY media production *Shejay* focuses on the significant contributions that a diverse range of women are making to EDM cultural production. Such DIY media productions can thus have a far-reaching, positive impact on women and girls.

Consequently, women in EDM are using the web as a tool to increase their visibility in a culture where men consistently overshadow them. Here, they have control over the content they create and post. *Shejay* is one of the longest running e-zines dedicated entirely

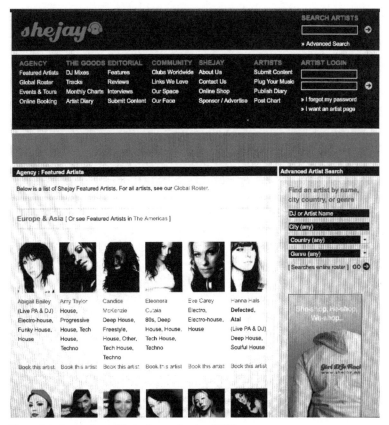

Figure 3.4: Screenshot of *Shejay* featured artists (2011).

to women in EDM. Launched in 2001 and still active as of this writing, for years its mission statement explained that its 'reason for being derives from a need to create a home. A group of inspired individuals were on the hunt for a dwelling that supports women who thrive and live in the world of electronic music'. An updated 'About Us' section with the heading 'The Shejay Mission' now reads:

> Shejay is the world's largest online roster & ezine of female DJs and artists in the dance music scene. Firmly established as the go-to place for promoters looking for female talent, Shejay's Global Roster proudly houses over 1800 women from every corner [of] the globe.
>
> The site also plays hostess to worldwide event listings, reviews, interviews and articles focusing on dance music and also features a slew of charts, DJ mixes and original tracks from our artists.
>
> Shejay has reigned supreme as the … Queen of all things female in dance music since 2001. With the word 'Shejay' now commonly used by journalists and promoters the world over to describe a female DJ, it's safe to say Shejay has played a pioneering role in helping to give these women both a face and a place on the map.
>
> But it wouldn't be any of this without the artists, contributors and a small team of dedicated people.

The 'dedicated people' listed below this text on the site are referred to as 'The Shejay Mafia', and consist of the ten individuals primarily responsible for managing the site and its offerings. Co-founders Kelly Sylvia and Mona Holmes are based in London and Los Angeles respectively, with the remainder of the team hailing from major cities around the globe including Toronto, Canada; Berlin, Germany; Dublin, Ireland; and Delhi, India. As the site's 'About Us' section outlines, *Shejay* fulfills the functions of traditional, print-based EDM magazines through its focus on event listings, reviews, interviews and other articles. However, the site goes further and also functions as a booking agency. It provides a place for women to upload information about themselves, including their geographical location and EDM genre of choice, which could lead to promoters booking them for DJ events.

Several women expressed a preference for working with female booking agents and promoters whenever possible to minimize problems of sexual harassment, lack of payment, and being booked simply because they were women. DJ Barbarella [Barbara Mayers] described an experience that led to her conscious decision to work with other women.

> I had a booking agent in Chicago who was part of some roster[4] as a DJ. He kept telling promoters that I was his girlfriend so promoters would book us in the same hotel room; it was really frustrating. Assault happens, it happens more than it should. Put drugs and alcohol in the picture and forget it, so that was really frustrating. I don't like having things assumed about me because I'm a woman, like I'm gonna give you a blow job, or you can

pay me less. I have a booking agent [now], she's from Iowa, she lives in Des Moines. She's really cool, she's tough.

(DJ Barbarella, 23 May 2003 interview)

Given such experiences, *Shejay*'s booking services provide women with an alternative to working with men in an environment where it can be difficult to find female booking agents and promoters. Because the 'Shejay Mafia' team includes booking managers for the Americas, Europe, and Asia, the site presents DJs and producers with international networking opportunities should they choose to upload their bios to the site for promoters to access.

In addition to a constantly changing page of 'featured artists', *Shejay* features a 'Global Roster' section that provides names, locations, subgenre interests, biographies, contact information, pictures and websites of its members. Such a space is especially useful for women who do not have their own websites, but it can also benefit artists with personal web pages, who can increase traffic to their sites by linking them to their *Shejay* bios.

Women are encouraged to upload their own bios and pics on the site where they have the freedom to choose how they want to be represented. Of course, similar to the DJs in Chapter 2, the norms of EDM culture narrowly define their options if they want to be accepted in EDM DJ circles. Thus, based on their pictures the majority of the hundreds of DJs featured overwhelmingly conform to the sex kitten and t-shirt DJ personas. Nonetheless, because *Shejay*'s management consists of a global team, the site features a diverse range of women with respect to race, ethnicity and nationality from every part of the globe. Most of the bios emphasize musical credentials, accomplishments and influences.

Filling in a void left by mainstream EDM magazines and trade publications, *Shejay*'s editorial pages feature the accomplishments of female artists and future EDM opportunities. Stories focus on topics such as record labels searching for new producers, the experiences of women starting their own record labels and in-depth interviews with accomplished female DJs and producers. In the spirit of Riot Grrrl culture, *Shejay* also encourages its readers to become active contributors to the site. The 'Submit Content' page reads, 'Did you know you *don't* have to be a member, a journalist or even a girl to publish content on Shejay's editorial pages? Fer [sic] serious! Anyone can get involved and be heard in lots of different ways.' In this respect, the site's intention is to stimulate dialogue about issues relevant to women in EDM while being inclusive of male perspectives and male-generated content. It is noteworthy that *Shejay*'s operations are less hierarchical than those of any EDM print publications, where only the writings of a select group of people are published. This is due both to *Shejay*'s interest in publishing diverse content and its need for a constant, fresh supply of content to remain relevant and encourage readers to visit the site regularly.

However, unlike the Riot Grrrls, who intentionally rejected corporate media and its practices, *Shejay* welcomes corporate sponsorship. At the time of this writing in 2011 the site did not appear to have any sponsors though it did feature an advertisement for a remix contest in 2010. Thus, despite the site's interest in advertising it seemingly generates little advertising revenue. Its inability to pay contributors is yet another reason why readers are encouraged to become content providers. Nonetheless, doing so provides further opportunity for alternative, public representations of women in EDM that emphasize their musical interests, skills and accomplishments. Overall, the diverse representations and narratives assembled from women's perspectives featured in *Shejay* serve as a discursive intervention in EDM and DJ culture; such publications also offer women additional opportunities to network and increase their professional visibility.

Conclusion

Women have invested a great deal of time and effort in creating women-centred EDM spaces. The monthly potluck held in Portland, Oregon; the Internet mailing list Sisterdjs and the e-zine *Shejay* demonstrate the types of networks women have developed in response to the male-centricity of EDM and DJ culture and the poor representation of women in EDM and commercial culture. While each is unique, these spaces have similar purposes, goals and outcomes. Mainly, they all strive to increase the networking potential, subcultural capital and overall visibility of women in EDM.

The Portland potlucks were particularly successful in encouraging local women to meet face-to-face to explore possibilities for DJ events and other ways to magnify the visibility of female DJs in the area. These face-to-face meetings represent the only networking opportunity discussed here that also provided direct and immediate feedback for new DJs, through the opportunity to practice their mixing skills under Layla's guidance. Despite DJ culture's rootedness in location, the Internet – and the Sister PDX mailing list in particular – was a significant tool used to promote the monthly potlucks and related events.

Similarly, but operating solely online, the Sisterdjs mailing list was established as a resource to promote the professional growth of women DJs worldwide. The list's content reflects women's willingness to share information and personal experiences as a means of providing and receiving support. The dialogue generated by the list was valuable on two levels. It increased participants' subcultural capital with respect to equipment care and subgenre interests, and it also enhanced their bridging social capital, as they now had more people to turn to for advice and information about EDM and DJ culture.

The e-zine *Shejay* is the most formal of the spaces considered in this chapter. In addition to providing networking opportunities for women DJs themselves, it also promotes a *public* image of women in EDM. In doing so it moves beyond generating capital and networking to presenting alternative representations of women that focus on their EDM skills and interests. Internet technologies have thus provided key tools for generating women-centred EDM spaces, increasing women's networking potential and encouraging more women to become active in EDM culture as DJs and producers.

Nonetheless, much work remains to be done. In a club culture where men still hold most of the power, it is understandable that many women fear creating more distance between men and women by labeling themselves feminists, despite their feminist actions. Contrary to popular discourse that presents feminism as passé, this chapter demonstrates a continued need for feminist politics and action. To move beyond women-centred spaces and penetrate higher profile EDM communities and outlets, women must continue to support and network with one another. Expanding their knowledge base and networks can not only lead to more subcultural and in turn economic capital, but it can also create more pleasurable experiences for women in EDM. Furthermore, growth in the visibility of women in EDM expands the possibilities for women's interests and participation far beyond this context. It also works to break down barriers and assumptions about women's relationships to not only music but also other technology-related practices. Continuing this discussion, the following chapter presents a case study of the intricacies and inner workings of the Sister USA DJ collective, examining in depth the establishment, maintenance and dissolution of the longest-running women-centred DJ collective in the United States.

Notes

1. Jungle's defining musical characteristics are its use of accelerated, chopped-up breakbeat rhythms (the percussion-only section of funk or disco tracks) and heavy bass lines. Otherwise known as drum 'n' bass, this style of EDM emerged in the 1990s when the influence of British B-boys, reggae and hip hop culture made their way into the United Kingdom rave scene (Reynolds 1999).
2. PDX is the airport code for Portland, Oregon.
3. For examples, see http://www.forestgreen.org; http://www.djdenise.com; http://www.djamber.com.
4. The term roster refers to a collection of DJs, often affiliated with a particular booking agency.

Chapter 4

Building a Women-Centred DJ Collective: From San Francisco
to Cyberspace to Sister USA

It is close to midnight by the time I get to the club in San Francisco's SoMa district. Once inside, I am surprised by the sheer magnitude of the space: three stories of thumping bass beats emanating from the club's four dance floors. Besides a sophisticated light set-up, the main dance floor also includes four huge projection screens and a liquid, LED-lit 'waterfall wall'. The club is close to capacity and the anticipation on the dance floor is palpable as the next DJ steps up behind the turntables.

I have been to clubs like this before, packed with people dancing on Saturday nights, in several cities across North America and Western Europe. But this event is different. The DJ about to play is the first of the three headliners for the night – and all three are women. It was 30 April 2005 and the main event featured England's DJ Rap (discussed in Chapter 2), with opening acts by DJ Amber and Queen Agnes B, two local San Francisco DJs and Sister SF residents.[1]

As earlier chapters suggest, by the mid-2000s women in San Francisco had managed to carve out a space for themselves in EDM culture in ways that had yet to happen elsewhere. In this city it was common to see women DJing at clubs or shopping in local record stores strewn with flyers advertising their upcoming events. To a large extent, the strong presence of women in San Francisco's EDM culture stemmed from the efforts of Sister SF, a local women-centred DJ collective.

This chapter explores Sister SF's identity-establishing practices, philosophical positions and impact on women DJs and EDM culture more broadly. As the longest-running women-centred DJ collective in the United States (1997–2007), its far-reaching impact culminated in the formation of additional chapters throughout the country – including Sister PDX, discussed in Chapter 3 – that were loosely bound together as part of the Sister USA network.

To contextualize Sister SF's perspectives and actions, the chapter begins with an overview of several women-centred media collectives that have existed over the years. These include the Womyn's Music movement of the 1970s, the Riot Grrrl movement of the 1990s and various radio and television broadcasting collectives beginning in 1969. It then relates Sister SF's origin story and delves into the specifics of its decade-long practices and eventual dissolution. In line with the politics of the DJs and producers interviewed, as a collective Sister SF publicly rejected the label 'feminist' even as it embodied feminist practices. As I argue in detail below, a central factor contributing to the group's visibility and longevity was the unique ways in which it implemented DIY practices and philosophies in tandem with more commercial/corporate strategies. Thus, it is useful to begin by looking back on the women-centred DIY media efforts that preceded Sister SF.

DIY media collectives

The term DIY can be traced back to the punk rock ideology of the 1980s that was rooted in a commitment to self-reliance. In her study of the evolution of indie culture Kaya Oakes describes the punk rock music scene of the time as one 'which was a self-operating, self-navigating subculture with its own set of ideals and alternative models for doing business' (Oakes 2009: 44). In her book *DIY: The Rise of Lo-Fi Culture* Amy Spencer (2008) presents a broader description of DIY when she writes:

> The DIY movement is about using anything you can get your hands on to shape your own cultural entity: your own version of whatever you think is missing in mainstream culture. You can produce your own zine, record an album, publish your own book – the enduring appeal of this movement is that anyone can be an artist or creator. The point is to get involved.
>
> (11)

For decades, women in various locations with a range of experiences have been motivated to create women-centred, DIY media collectives that reflect their ideas and bring visibility to cultural elements and issues they feel are overlooked in mainstream culture. One reason such groups have emerged is to counter the gender inequality found at most levels of media production, including the music and broadcasting industries. They recognize the importance of maintaining control over their productions in order to present voices and opinions that challenge dominant ideological assumptions about women, both within and beyond these industries.

With respect to music, both the Riot Grrrl movement of the 1990s and the Womyn's Music movement of the 1970s embraced a DIY sensibility. Significantly, however, the Riot Grrrl movement was compromised by mainstream media outlets. Despite their best efforts to maintain an identity that opposed and openly critiqued dominant culture, Riot Grrrl was quickly co-opted by it. Mainstream music journalists, attempting to define the meaning of these new girl-centric activities for themselves and their readers, oversimplified and distorted the movement to fit their agendas by linking it explicitly to radical feminism (Gottlieb and Wald 1994) and presenting its pro-female attitude as anti-male (Kearney 1997). Even more problematically, popular culture quickly absorbed and repackaged the language and style of Riot Grrrl into a superficial form of 'girl power' that was promoted via consumer goods (Bleyer 2004). As Reynolds and Press (1996) explain:

> By early '93, many of the Riot Grrrls felt the scene had been mediatised out of existence, misrepresented and trivialized; some refused to use the term to describe themselves, because it had so rapidly become a free floating signifier circulating through media hyperspace.
>
> (324)

In an effort to maintain control over their image Riot Grrrls responded by refusing interviews with the music press (Raphael 1996), as the following notice in the zine Hair Pie #2:1 indicates:

> I've noticed (as I'm sure you have) riot grrl is getting more press (daily star) for fuck's sake, we've gotta stay underground and undermine the corporate rock press by doing it ourselves so we can talk about our beliefs to people without fear of being misunderstood or the truth being distorted.
>
> (as cited in Leonard 1997: 244)

In a 1994 interview, Niki from Huggy Bear explained,

> We recognised early on that the journalist/popstar dialogue is a complex system of mythologies and identifications to do with fake hierarchies which connect preferences of desirability via the kinds of photos which are used to represent you or how much space is given to each member of a band in an interview.
>
> (Raphael 1996: 161)

In other words, Riot Grrrl bands opted to cut themselves off from the mainstream music press because they recognized that they did not have control over their images in these contexts. Instead, the press personnel in charge of conducting interviews and photo shoots had complete control over how Riot Grrrls were represented in their publications. Similar to the networking examples discussed in Chapter 3, Sister SF's efforts have remained under the radar of the mainstream press. The group's anonymity among music journalists along with a set of key strategic moves enabled Sister SF to maintain a strong hold over its identity.

Furthermore, Norma Coates (1997) discusses the Riot Grrrl's loss of control over their own representation as a primary factor that contributed to the enduring position of women 'on the gendered margins of rock' (55). This argument applies not only to rock but also to women in most other popular music genres. Women's lack of industry power, notably in areas that include journalism, management and music production contribute to this marginalization and are the subjects of Chapter 5.

To some extent the Riot Grrrls' DIY philosophies of the 1990s can in fact be traced back to the more radical, lesbian Womyn's Music movement that began in the 1970s (Kearney 1997) and expanded women's opportunities in popular music. Both groups stressed the importance of women-owned and operated record labels and control over representation (Wald 1998) and sound (Sandstrom 2000).

Over time, women in broadcasting dealt with struggles that paralleled those of women in the music industry. Public broadcasting, like music, is a male-centred media space in which women have actively sought to create alternative sites of media practice. In response to men's dominance in the industry, a host of women-centred media projects have materialized since the second wave of the feminist movement – some brief, others more long-term – to counter the gender inequality found at most levels of media production (Mitchell 2000a, 2000b; Women's Airwaves Survey 2000; Carter 2004; Steiner 2005).

Feminist radio programming was first introduced in the United States in 1969 on WBAI in New York (Steiner 1992 as cited in Mitchell 2000b). According to Susan Carter (2004), a total of 17 women's radio collectives existed in the United States and Canada at the height of the second wave of the feminist movement in the early 1970s; these groups frequently communicated with one another, usually by newsletter. Although they all worked to introduce women's voices and issues on the air, the degree to which they identified their projects as feminist varied from site to site.

Both the Riot Grrrl and Womyn's Music movements were DIY enterprises intended to appeal to niche audiences, most of whom embraced feminism to some degree. Alternatively, because of the very nature of public broadcasting, much of the content on women's radio and public television programmes was meant to both challenge dominant ideological assumptions and invite a broader listening or viewing audience. Linda Steiner's (2005) work on a group of women in New Jersey who produced a feminist public affairs series called *New Directions for Women* (*NDW*), cablecast on cable television public access channels, explores this challenge. The group had an explicit feminist agenda in its programming, which it believed was relevant to men despite having little evidence of who was tuning in. Although not without its struggles, the programme premiered in 1994 and was still on the air at the time of Steiner's writing, though the producers were questioning both its audience and impact on social and political change.

Women's programmes on local radio, where sexism has often been an issue (Women's Airwaves Survey 2000), have typically had much shorter life spans. An analysis of BBC Radio in 1983 found numerous instances in which men belittled and objectified women in the studio. The few women on the air at the time were assigned to 'lighter' areas of programming and male broadcasters used language that alienated women and reinforced sexist attitudes. In response to this treatment, a number of women-centred community radio stations, many of them short-lived, were established to challenge mainstream representations of women in the United Kingdom and the United States. Most of the stations had feminist aims, but participants made the conscious decision not to label them as such for fear of alienating potential listeners (Mitchell 2000a).

Similarly, while Sister SF was established to introduce the efforts of female DJs into EDM culture, it also took measures to distance itself from feminism. Yet Sister SF employs women's programming strategies to create an environment that not only highlights the talents of female DJs, but also enables them to flourish in public settings. Fortunately, the ubiquity of personal computers and the Internet has enabled women and girls to participate in public discourse on their own terms (Garrison 2000; Koerber 2001; Pomerantz, Currie and Kelly 2004; Kearney 2006) in ways that were not available to their predecessors.

Establishing women-centred DJ spaces

This case study brings together and expands upon several of the themes discussed in earlier chapters by examining Sister SF's technological and social practices, as well as the struggles it faced over the course of its ten-year history. Though numerous women-centred DJ collectives came and went during the period of Sister SF's existence, it was the longest running collective of its kind in the United States. Several of the most well-known female DJs in the Bay Area were members of Sister SF at some point in their careers. In the early 2000s the collective grew to include additional chapters, first in Portland (Sister PDX), followed by New York City (Sister NYC) and Denver (Sister DEN). The expansion of the collective to other United States cities was indicative of Sister SF's widespread impact and the progress it made towards its goal of establishing a nationwide collective known as Sister USA.

Sister SF sprung from a female DJ collective that started in 1993. Every Thursday night a group of women would spin together at an event they called 'Your Sister's House'. Over time, the night started to earn a reputation in the city. Polywog [Rebecca Corbett], one of the founding members of both Your Sister's House and Sister SF, explained the impetus for these early events:

> It's about allowing these parties to give these women a chance because at that time, especially trying to break into the rave scene there was no way we would have gotten a gig there. Men would have just laughed at you because it was a time when people were emerging. DJing was still kinda new, a new career path [that was] hard to break in, so this was an opportunity to play, to get heard and it was really fun.
>
> (Polywog, 16 May 2005 interview)

Your Sister's House was the first female DJ crew in the city. At its helm was Liz Roberts, who was not a DJ but organized and coordinated the collective's events. According to Polywog, the weekly parties 'start[ed] pulling some heavyweight energy for women in the scene'. Your Sister's House lasted from 1993 to 1995 and included Liz Roberts, Charlotte the Baroness, DRC, Polywog, Shana Kleyman, Susan 28 and Dani (http://www.aboutus.org/Sistersf.com).

It was during a 1997 interview for Berkeley radio station KPFA that Polywog thought it was the right time to bring back a female DJ crew.

> I remember being at this friend's house. Linzee was there and this new girl Siren who had all this energy, I could just tell, she was like I'm gonna DJ. I was talking to them and said why don't we get a female DJ thing going. I can help you get press.
>
> (Polywog, 16 May 2005 interview)

Polywog went on to explain that Linzee and DJ Siren were instrumental in bringing back the collective in 1997 while Polywog herself was on tour, first with the Lollapalooza music festival and later opening for the band Jane's Addiction. The timing was right in part because EDM's popularity in the United States was beginning to peak. In deciding what to name the new collective, the women agreed it should honour Your Sister's House in such a way that this second incarnation would be seen as an extension of the original. Linzee [Lynn Butta] said that it was during a brainstorming session that she proposed Sister. 'I was like, "How about Sister?" It was my idea to do different cities. "Let's call it Sister SF." This was way before we had different chapters.' Soon after, XJS [Annie Shaw] – who in Polywog's words was 'phenomenal' – came along and took charge of the collective. The original Sister SF lineup included the San Francisco DJs XJS, Siren, Linzee, Polywog and Charlotte the Baroness.

At the time Linzee was neither an MC nor a DJ, but an aspiring music journalist, who covered the electronic music scene for local publications and befriended several of the city's early female DJs. It was not until Sister SF got off the ground that she began to MC for Sister SF events, but even from the sidelines she noticed that women

> would go to step up to the decks next and then the guy would not even quickly go over the mixer, [which is] the courteous thing to do. Every mixer's different. It doesn't mean you don't know how to use a mixer, [it's] just a nice thing to do … [you] still get assholes but it was really bad [before], where they would almost sabotage you.
>
> (Linzee, 14 May 2005 interview)

This is just one example of the treatment aspiring female DJs received from men. The formation of Sister SF emerged from the experiences of female Bay Area DJs, who recognized that they could accomplish much more and gain greater respect working together than they could individually. Linzee's transition into MCing is a good example of how women-centred spaces encourage women to become producers of media, art and culture in ways they might not otherwise have been inclined to do.

Linzee spoke at length about the experiences that set her on her path to MCing:

> How the whole MC thing came along, we were doing this party when drum 'n' bass was really hot, like '97 when it was really going on. Had this all-female lineup. Our parties always had a certain vibe. Our thing was always, 'Wow, they've got a really good vibe.' Everyone was freaking out. 'Who are these girls? They're all in one room totally having fun.' So that was really cool. There was a microphone there. Everyone was freaking out. They'd never seen these girls before. I wanted everyone to know who they were so I got on the microphone just announcing stuff. This is Sister and you're listening to this DJ right now. I started listening, going out to drum 'n' bass parties, really getting wrapped up in it so at every party I was more and more rapping and MCing to the music. I was always doing poetry and I'm a writer too so it was kinda like a progression. So I started doing that for a while and then I started taking voice lessons. It's kinda because of Sister that that

Figure 4.1: MC Linzee on the mic (2002).
Photographer: Kimberly Howard.

happened. I had a platform, I was able to do it and they were letting me, [saying] 'That's really cool, keep doing that'.

(Linzee, 14 May 2005 interview)

As Linzee's experience illustrates, the collective created an environment of open communication and support where experience and information were freely circulated. This was something its members had not experienced previously in the local DJ scene. Yet they did not publicly frame their mission as a feminist or in any other way as a political undertaking.

'We're not raging feminists'

In 2005, Sister SF consisted of ten members. The collective's eight DJs included DJ Amber, Forest Green, J-Fi, Melyss, Queen Agnes B, Polywog, Samira and Seraphim. Audio Angel was the group's sole MC, and XJS had recently stepped down from DJing but remained a

Figure 4.2: Sister SF members, as featured on the front page of Sister SF's website, www.sistersf.com (2007). Photographer: Charlotte Fiorito.

member in an advisory role. All of the women were in their 20s and 30s at the time. They are all white with the exception of Audio Angel, who is African-American. Similar to the actions of the Detroit Women's Radio Workshop in the early 1970s, the collective held monthly meetings in which members reviewed their recent activities, delegated responsibilities and organized upcoming events. In addition to their Sister SF commitments, all of the members had full- or part-time work obligations and several belonged to other DJ crews.

To some extent Sister SF self-identified more by what the group was not than by what it was. Although it embodied feminist goals and a pro-woman standpoint, the collective openly rejected a feminist label. Its mission statement illustrated the group's conflicted relationship to feminism, which mirrored that of women's radio stations in the United Kingdom (Mitchell 2000a) and women's collective radio programming in the United States as far back as the 1970s (Carter 2004).

The following mission statement served the collective for its entire duration:

SISTER is a place for female DJs to get gigs without bias, providing a supportive, friendly platform for any female DJ, MC or live performer to enjoy their music where gender is not an issue ... a place where women are neither fighting to be heard nor imported merely to fulfill a gimmick quotient. We're not raging feminists – we just think it's better to be viewed as a DJ first, and then as a woman, when you're behind the decks.

SISTER is not anti-male at all, it is simply pro-female.

The collective's opposition to feminism is not surprising given the historical context in which the group was established. As discussed in previous chapters, by the mid-1990s the feminist backlash that began in the 1980s (Faludi 1991) was well under way. Evidence of a backlash within women-centred media collectives appears as early as 1978, when WOMN first went on the air in New Haven, Connecticut. It was the first radio station to identify as a 'woman's station' after the second wave feminist movement. Despite the station's feminist content, WOMN's management team purposefully avoided giving the station a feminist label so as not to offend any potential listeners (Carter 2004).

Nevertheless, according to WOMN's vice president, it was the station's feminist content that led to its downfall within its first year (Carter 2004). Although the owner and vice president of WOMN were men, research shows that women in comparable positions tended to make similar decisions not to label their content as feminist. In 1982, the women-run station WWMN-AM went on the air in Flint, Michigan. Although like WOMN it was not explicitly feminist, it too went under after only seven months on the air.

Women involved in women's radio stations in the United Kingdom in the 1990s – such as Fem FM in Bristol – also consciously decided not to label their stations 'feminist' for fear of estranging listeners. Mitchell (2000a) claims that this was true of most of the stations at the time because women were so anxious not to alienate men. However, there were also women programmers and listeners for whom the labels 'feminism' and 'feminist' were problematic. The first full-time commercial station in the United Kingdom aimed at women was called Viva! According to Mitchell (2000a), 'competing discourses of feminism and femininity surrounded the station' (107). Awarded a licence in June 1994, Viva! was on the air from July 1995 until November 1996. Audience research found that women would listen to Viva! as long as its content was not overtly feminist or anti-male, but technical problems and lack of funding, as well as poor programming and music choices, all led to its failure.

The contradiction in Sister SF's mission statement speaks further to the persuasiveness of the feminist backlash. These women claimed they were 'not fighting to be heard' despite forming a collective based on the inequalities and the silencing they experienced as EDM DJs. The final sentence of the mission statement emphasizes this point. It is positioned on its own, separate from the rest of the paragraph, to emphasize to readers that 'SISTER is not anti-male'. That the group feels compelled to make such an overt claim illustrates their concerns about coming across as feminist, regardless of their individual politics. That concern clearly stems from popular misconceptions of what it means to be a feminist, that is that feminists are enraged and man-hating.

In other words, Sister SF's mission statement speaks more to contemporary society's discomfort with and misunderstanding of feminism than it does to the practices of the collective. In this sense the statement can be read as a precautionary measure. As with many women who engaged in activities supporting women, these women feel compelled to distance themselves from popular misconceptions about feminism in order to safeguard the longevity of their collective – regardless of whether they are aware of the demise of earlier women's media collectives that adopted a feminist stance. In her analysis of women's access to radio, Carter concludes, 'although the voice can be female, the message cannot be gendered feminist if the voice is to remain viable' (2004: 180). Thus, by adopting a pro-female stance that is nevertheless distanced from feminism, Sister SF strategically minimized the potential alienation of prospective fans, booking agents, club owners and other men and women who might be driven away by the feminist label.

The detailed pages of the collective's website sistersf.com, which was online from 1997 to 2007, illustrated the group's commitment to feminist ideology and practice despite its disavowals. Clearly, Sister SF was dedicated to maintaining a women-centred DJ space to provide women DJs access to the information, practices and spaces that typically were (and continue to be) much more accessible to men. In addition to showcasing current Sister SF residents, the site functioned as an encyclopedia on EDM and DJ culture. It also made available information rich in subcultural capital that is generally shared selectively and thus reserved for people 'in the know'.

A noteworthy example was the availability of sample booking contracts on the site for anyone's perusal. In addition, the 'Guest DJs' section included the bios of over 70 women from around the world. For the novice to EDM culture and/or DJing the site also provided an extensive database of in-group terminology and definitions that are usually learned gradually, via long-term participation in the culture. Both the quality and quantity of information available on the site helped to create a space committed to increasing the presence of women in EDM DJ culture through knowledge dissemination, education and networking. Collectively, these features reflect a feminist practice by empowering women in EDM culture. By providing a space in which women can write themselves into DJ culture via their bios and exchange life experiences with other women in the network, Sister SF provided women with the language and knowledge needed to intervene in EDM culture, which historically has paid little mind to the efforts of women DJs.

In addition, areas of the site that offered resource sharing and DJ profiles encouraged communication between individuals and groups across geographical boundaries. Such practices provided valuable networking opportunities for members and non-members alike. In the words of XJS [Annie Shaw], the Sister SF site stood out among the thousands of DJ websites because:

Most DJ sites out there are not set up for sharing information; I mean that's not the point of them at all. I think that it is pretty unusual for a site to share contracts and as much information and help as you need … we're not just promoting ourselves, we're trying to share information, we're trying to build up other woman DJs, like here put your bio on our site. Altruism is not a key word in the DJ scene at all, it's really like 'no, me first' normally, plus we're promoting a gender instead of a genre.

(XJS, 22 July 2003 interview)

XJS's comments could be interpreted as contradicting the mission statement's anti-feminist position. Whereas the mission statement makes a point of stating that a DJ's sex or gender is not as important as her DJ skills, XJS stresses that Sister SF is promoting a gender instead of a particular genre of music. Promoting the activities and skills of women in EDM is central to Sister SF's agenda. The contradiction between XJS's statement and the collective's mission statement signals a tension often experienced by women in male-dominated spaces. Women in EDM experience a conflict similar to that faced by women in rock. Many artists shun the label 'women in rock' despite recognizing instances in which their gender had an undeniable impact on their professional experiences (Carson, Lewis and Shaw 2004). Many women in popular music – whether rock, EDM or other genres – aspire to work in an environment in which gender is irrelevant to their experiences. Yet it is precisely because of the continued existence of gendered power dynamics that collectives like Sister SF exist.

DIY goals and underpinnings

As noted above, Sister SF embodied elements of both DIY and mainstream commercial culture that are often viewed as antithetical to one another. However, Sister SF members attribute the collective's success to its incorporation of practices from both of these cultures. For example, when asked what she liked best about being a member of Sister SF, DJ Amber [Amber Nixon] replied:

There's a lot of things that are attractive about being part of the collective. What I like best about it is that it has such a polished and clean and professional image … we spend a huge amount of time being a resource on our website and working to promote other DJs, not just us. In the end it ends up coming back to us.

(DJ Amber, 16 July 2003 interview)

Amber's response highlights the benefits for Sister SF members of merging the philosophies and practices of DIY community and mainstream professional culture. She values the group's professionalism and polished image that is typical of corporate culture and her conclusion that 'it ends up coming back to us' alludes to the recognition Sister SF had gained for women DJs in the larger EDM community.

Sister SF's commitment to a DIY ethic was evident in the collective's dedication to creating alternative spaces both on- and offline that heightened the visibility of women DJs. Sister's efforts can be described as creating another node in what Doreen Piano (2003) refers to as a 'subcultural infrastructure'. Piano (2003) defines this infrastructure as comprising post-Riot Grrrl, DIY cottage industries that include the production of goods as diverse as music, zines, soap and alternative menstrual products.

A key element of Sister SF's subcultural infrastructure was hosting events that featured female DJs[2] in an effort to promote their visibility. In addition, members organized fundraising events for local non-profits, and even hosted free DJ clinics where they taught the basics of DJing to beginners, who could benefit from their expertise. Traces of Sister SF's influence are mapped throughout this book. As discussed in Chapter 3, Layla Dudley credited Sister SF and its Internet presence with inspiring her to start a women-centred DJ collective in Portland, Oregon. In her words, 'I sat down and got to talking with them in 2001 … I was inspired by them … I'd been surfing the web for female collectives. I went onto Google and punched in female DJs or something like that' (Layla, 13 July 2003 interview). Layla's account speaks to the significance and impact of groups like Sister SF on aspiring media artists looking to form connections with more established peers.

Online, the collective freely distributes 'insider' information, lists helpful resources and posts information-rich articles on topics such as 'Making a CD', 'Promoting Events' and 'Forming a DJ Crew', all of which encourage networking and more active participation in DJ culture through grass-roots practices. Sister SF's inclusion of a 'bios' section on its website further illustrates its commitment to helping all female DJs regardless of whether they are members of the collective. When we met in 2003, San Jose resident DJ Ara [Heather Reagan] claimed that she invested little effort in promoting herself. Nonetheless, when given the opportunity she posted a guest page on Sister SF's website that led to valuable networking opportunities and even an out-of-state booking in Texas. In her words:

> The site has been the key; I got my first out-of-state gig from someone who was cruising the Sister SF site who wanted a Trance DJ, so they e-mailed me. At first I thought it was a joke so I didn't email him back. I asked all my friends, 'What should I tell him I charge?' So I had a friend who's been traveling doing DJing and he's like, 'Just tell him you play for this much and they have to pay your airfare and hotel.' I thought it was a long shot. He's going to say no way because I didn't have that much of a background. Then he emailed me back, 'OK, do you have an agreement?' and then I thought, 'Oh my gosh, I really have to have something.' So I got the agreement off the Sister website and tailored it and I got the gig in El Paso, Texas. It was amazing. It was the best party I've ever played at.
>
> (DJ Ara, 20 July 2003 interview)

Because she did not expect to have the opportunity to play paid DJ gigs out-of-state, DJ Ara had not acquired the necessary insider information to create a booking contract. Her experiences demonstrate the far-reaching impact of collectives like Sister SF in helping women transition to the more professional levels of DJing.

Sister SF recognized that because the overwhelming majority of booking agents, event managers and club owners in DJ culture are men, it was imperative to present an image that would appeal to both men and women. Also, because rave culture in the United States began to decline after 2000, Sister SF's members knew that to remain viable they had to represent themselves and the collective in ways that resonated with the mainstream club culture. Consequently, Sister SF adopted strategies that enabled the collective to preserve its politics while presenting a professional, non-threatening image. Unlike Riot Grrl zines (Kearny 2006) or politically alternative news media that 'eschew a glossy, sophisticated look on both philosophical and practical grounds' (Steiner 2004: 318), Sister SF was as deeply committed to maintaining a polished, branded image typical of commercial/corporate culture as it was to achieving the goals discussed above. The following section examines the details of the collective's branding practices as they have been implemented both off- and online.

Branding practices

In his discussion of *Star Wars* fan culture, Henry Jenkins (2006) examines how advances in computer technology are enabling amateur film-makers to create films whose aesthetic qualities parallel those of big-budget Hollywood productions. Beyond film-making, amateurs of all kinds are ever more able to create media texts that aesthetically mirror corresponding items that are professionally created. This dynamic is especially apparent in web design. As with amateur film-making, increased access to computer technologies and advanced web design skills enable DIY enterprises like Sister SF to create quality, visually interesting websites that resemble corporate/commercial sites dedicated to branding their products or services. By presenting its DIY practices and goals within the frame of a glossy, professional website, Sister SF heightened its professional aesthetic and thereby further legitimized the group.

In 2005, Sister SF's site received over 35,000 hits per month. In January 2007 a Google search for 'female DJ crew' returned sistersf.com as the first search hit, despite a decline in the collective's activities and the increasing proliferation of female DJs and crews at the time. Whereas prior to the explosion of digital technologies and tools a DIY zine was easily distinguishable from a glossy, professionally created print magazine, advanced web design tools and skills have blurred the lines between cottage industries and commercial productions.

Since the 1990s, scholars, marketing strategists and activists have discussed the role and significance of branding. A concern with how to operationalize and manage brands has been at the forefront of management studies (Murphy 1987; Aaker 1991; Kapferer 1997; Davis 2002; Davis, Dunn and Aaker 2002), with a growing focus on how to implement global branding strategies (Wright 2002; Rozin and Magnusson 2003; Holt, Quelch and Taylor 2004). Branding is generally discussed in academic and popular literature in relation to commercial culture and the powerful images and strategies adopted by corporations to market and sell their goods. This shift in emphasis from manufacturing goods to marketing them has been well documented. However, thus far much less attention has been paid to the impact of what Naomi Klein (1997) calls the 'scaling-up of the logo's role' (28) on cultural production outside the commercial environment in which it first flourished.

Despite the proliferation of advertising, logos and branding in popular culture, little consideration has been given to the potential effects of branding techniques implemented by individuals, not-for-profits, (sub)cultural groups or other collectives, many of which are actively adopting professional techniques to advance their causes. The sheer pervasiveness of corporate marketing ensures that the general public – including members of Sister SF – are not only exposed to, but also actively buy into the value of successful marketing techniques, including branding.

While the incentives for creating brand identification in corporate culture are obvious – higher product sales and profitability – there are parallel as well as divergent motives for other types of groups to establish brand identity. Collectives such as Sister SF have appropriated branding techniques to demarcate, and in a sense advertise, their presence in the public sphere. Recall from Chapter 2 that the concept of branding is not a new phenomenon in EDM culture. Independent record labels have relied on branding a label's sound long before the 1990s (Hesmondhalgh 1998); however, what was an innovative beginning in the 1990s was the move to branding the identity of performers rather than shifts in style.

From its first days as a collective, Sister SF was committed to presenting a professional image complete with a consistent logo it publicized both offline and on the web. Over the years, as the website expanded, the general layout, colour scheme and logo remained consistent. Sister SF managed to maintain the site's consistency because it was designed by XJS, a member of the collective who was also a professional web designer. XJS applied the professional practices she learned as a corporate web designer to the collective's website. With extensive experience designing web pages for international corporations, XJS was well aware of the value of and return on long-term branding initiatives. As a result, she created an online presence for Sister SF that complemented the local identity she and the other members were establishing for the group in San Francisco.

As noted above, Sister SF's website content encouraged feminist practices such as resource sharing and community development. However, its polished appearance and the colour scheme of black, white and yellow enabled it to blend in with commercial DJ sites at that time, most notably those for high-profile dance clubs such as Crobar (www.crobar.com) and DJ equipment companies such as Technics (www.panasonic-europe.com/technics), Stanton (www.stantonmagnetics.com/v2/index.asp) and the Technics1200s Service Center (www.1200s.com), all of which favoured black, white and varying shades of grey as the basis for their colour schemes.

In her discussion of young female distro[3] owners, Kearney (2006) notes that most of the website designers she interviewed expressed femininity through the use of the colour pink, although a few chose to use black instead to create 'a serious or somber tone, and thus more masculine mood' (282). Given that most of the club managers and booking agents who hire DJs for paid gigs are men, it was in Sister SF's best interest for its site to embody an aesthetic that mirrored that of other professional EDM sites, such as the commercial websites for venues and gear discussed above.

Since the site's inception, XJS has maintained ownership of the Sister SF domain name. She designed, implemented and maintained the site to ensure brand – and in turn image – consistency. Sister SF was regularly updated and expanded, which helped it to generate ample traffic. Visitors to the site could read about upcoming gigs of Sister SF members, recent top ten track lists and join a listserv that distributed weekly event updates.

For years, XJS alone managed the site's design and content. While she continued to serve as the site's principal web designer throughout its existence, in its last few years she was assisted by fellow Sister SF member Samira [Samira Vijghen], also a professional web designer. Both women believed that the site's branded and professional image had been instrumental to the group's success. In Samira's words:

The site design and updates are best left in the hands of a few individuals. There's a recognizable look and feel to the crew and the branding and [XJS's] consistency and her drive to make things polished and really uniform-looking and consistent has been very integral to our success. You know, it's stuff that we talk about and it's stuff that will sometimes come up, 'cause more people want to have input on what the site looks like and how we present ourselves, and at the same time there's some real value there where you have, you look at the Sister logo and you just know. You look at the Sister site and it's been the same and people can expect that. It's a really important part of our identity.

(Samira, 20 May 2005 interview)

Figure 4.3: Sister SF logo. Designer: Annie Shaw.

By far, the site's most memorable feature is the web version of the Sister logo, which is prominently displayed in the top left corner at all times. It reads, 'Sister: women DJs and MCs in San Francisco and beyond.' A separate logo that simply spells out 'Sister SF' appears in banner form at the collective's events. The image portion of the web logo consists of a slender, female hand, working what appears to be an industry standard Technics turntable. The circular framing of the hand on the turntable and the absence of women's bodies in the design keeps the focus on the act of DJing itself.

Additional routine practices were employed to help ensure a consistent group identity. Sister SF residents claimed that XJS was not only the collective's principal web designer, but also the matriarch of the collective offline and ultimately the one who was 'holding the ship together' (Samira, 20 May 2005 interview). XJS was very particular about the events at which the Sister SF name and banner could be displayed. When members would DJ at events that were not officially produced or endorsed by the collective, the event and event holder's politics were discussed at a group meeting, where a decision was made regarding whether or not the banner should be displayed.

Sister beyond San Francisco

Sister SF was dedicated to expanding the presence of the collective and of female DJs in general across the United States, but its members were particular about the terms and conditions under which it happened. Over the years, Sister SF received numerous e-mails from women across the country wishing to start their own chapter of Sister after learning about the collective. As a result, practices were developed to maintain Sister's branded identity. According to XJS:

> We've also had discussions with other crews. Should we have random strangers using our name? Because we don't have a registered company, we don't have officialness. So it's always on the edge. We can prove use of the name and ownership of the logo but that doesn't mean a lot … so we've restricted it to people that we know.
>
> (XJS, 18 May 2005 interview)

Because no steps were ever taken to trademark the use of Sister in an EDM context, the group was very protective of its identity, which limited who they were willing to let organize under the Sister name. Thus, it was not enough for a group of women in a particular geographical location to express an interest in starting a chapter. Rather, members of potential chapters had to have some face-to-face contact with Sister SF prior to becoming official Sister members. Sister SF believed that having firsthand knowledge of the women who wanted to form Sister chapters was integral to ensuring that the purpose, politics and mission of new chapters followed those outlined by the original group.

Once members of Sister SF became aware of female DJ activity in Portland, they held face-to-face meetings to approve the official establishment of Sister PDX in 2002. Similar interactions led to the establishment of Sister DEN in Denver, Colorado in 2005. However, the most active chapter after Sister SF was Sister NYC, which started when a handful of San Francisco DJs moved to New York City. It was principally Linzee's move back to New York City that initiated the establishment of Sister NYC in 2002. In Linzee's words 'the whole reason why we started [Sister NYC] was because females weren't getting booked, they weren't getting exposed, anywhere' (Linzee, 14 May 2005 interview). The collective began organizing bi-weekly events to showcase the talents of its members. By the summer of 2005 they were so busy that they had to scale back considerably the number of events they organized. Linzee explained that quarterly Sister NYC parties became sufficient because the DJs were getting consistent bookings elsewhere.

To further protect its branded identity, Sister SF chose to maintain control over all chapters of Sister in cyberspace. According to XJS, the rationale was that managing the sites could help guarantee 'ultimate control' that 'the look and feel and philosophy [were] similar' (XJS, 22 July 2003 interview). To be able to supervise the sites, Sister SF retained ownership of the domain names of all Sister chapters and enforced the use of site templates that adhered to specific aesthetics that mirrored those of the original site. Such practices reflect the importance the group placed on retaining control over the images and politics of additional Sister chapters as they were launched. Overall, Sister SF used hierarchical strategies and consistent branding techniques typical of corporate/commercial culture to manage its expanding Sister USA network. These practices, which to some extent diverged from the group's altruistic actions and goals, functioned in tandem with the collective's community building practices.

Internship process

In contrast to the previous discussion of the relatively seamless integration of DIY and corporate practices, Sister SF's internship process is atypical in music scenes and illustrates a tension between these two sets of practices for the group offline. As the group's notoriety grew, female DJs were eager to join the collective. To deal with this increased interest Sister SF implemented an internship policy for potential new members. Their process was much more akin to the internship practices of commercial organizations than the membership practices of cottage industry collectives, which typically practice more inclusive community building strategies and less hierarchical approaches. Members of Sister SF reasoned that the process was vital to gauging the degree to which the work ethic, goals, attitudes, politics and commitment of interns matched their own.

Commenting on the evolution of the internship policy, XJS explained,

The intern process has sort of like changed over time. It started out being kind of like we get some people and they'll eventually be Sister residents, DJs, and in the meantime we'll see what they're made of by just, you know, making them do a bunch of shit work to see if they're up for it, whereas in the past we'd taken on residents – you were either a resident or not. So we decided that because we had a couple of DJs in the crew who didn't really fit in with the rest of the crew – it's like interviewing a roommate or a band member or something – that we had to like tighten it up a bit and get serious, you know, put some thought into the whole process a bit more.

(personal communication, 22 July 2003)

XJS's comments outline the ways in which Sister's internship process functioned in ways similar to the corporate process. Interns start out at the bottom, working for little or no recognition. Over time, if it appears that they are committed to and fit in with the group, they may be asked to stay on and move up to the next level, which in this case was recognition as an official Sister SF resident DJ. This practice is atypical in music communities, and especially so for women-centred music and broadcast media collectives. But for Sister SF it was viewed as a necessary step to ensure that the group maintained control over its image, politics and identity as it continued to expand.

Evolution and dissolution

From 1997 to 2007, Sister SF worked to heighten the visibility and influence of female EDM DJs. In the collective's own words, members sought to 'build up other women DJs' and promote 'a gender instead of a genre'. The Internet was a vital tool that Sister SF depended on to bring together its members and promote its growth. The creation of new media sites and networks is typical of both DIY culture and contemporary feminism. The creation of its own media sites both on- and offline enabled Sister SF to intervene in dominant discourses that present EDM culture as typically male, giving the impression that women are rarely present as artists in these spaces (Rodgers 2010). By breaking down the barriers between EDM consumers (such as record collectors, dancers and fans) and EDM producers (of events, cultural knowledge or websites), the collective democratized cultural production. Marian Bredin (1991) has argued that such democratization is vital to affirming the experiences of marginalization of women everywhere. In this way, Sister SF's practices exemplify feminist cultural politics in action.

In the latter half of the 2000s, both the Internet and Sister USA experienced significant growth and change. In 2005, XJS retired from DJing but continued to manage the Sister USA websites until 2006, when she handed the web design and management over to Samira. Concurrently, Sister NYC opted to break away from the Sister SF web design template. Linzee stated that Sister NYC wanted 'to take over the site so that it reflected New York. We wanted a new design and slightly different vibe' (Linzee, 14 May 2005 interview). In 2006, Sister NYC turned to a local graphic designer, Jennifer Wong, for a new look.[4]

By 2008, with the exception of Sister PDX, all of the Sister websites had been replaced with MySpace pages that advertised upcoming events. With over eight million artists and bands on MySpace (Owyang 2008), it is easy to understand why the collective felt that a MySpace presence was a better alternative than their individual websites, but the choice was not without some trade-offs. As DJ Amber explained at the time, 'MySpace is more the dominant place to hold your identity, but of course there's less that we can offer there' compared to the Sister websites (personal communication, 2 June 2008). While social networking sites like MySpace do not necessarily replace personal websites, they do provide an additional platform from which individuals and collectives like Sister USA can promote themselves and the efforts of women in a range of male-dominated media spaces. They are also easier and cheaper to update and maintain.

By 2008, Sister USA and all its chapters had become inactive. Commenting on its disintegration, DJ Amber emphasized the labour that Sister SF required of its residents.

> Sister SF was a lot of work. We met every month. We worked very hard. [We] put in time daily. It was almost like a company that we were running. It was a tremendous amount of work. We didn't have a new purpose … We didn't even really make a decision to conclude. It was such an amazing number of years. It would have been nice to go out with a bang. We're all still very close. Most of [us] are still DJing. [We've] just moved on.
> (personal communication, 5 January 2011)

Winter [Winter Clark], the co-founder of Sister NYC, similarly cited the achievement of its intended purpose as the central reason for Sister NYC's dissolution:

> It came to a close mainly because it fulfilled its ultimate purpose: to enable the members of Sister NYC and the females that came into contact with us to move forward and grow with their projects, ambitions and dreams they hoped to accomplish in the electronic music scene. Most of the original members went on to have successful DJing careers and founded record labels, released original music and traveled the world.
> (personal communication, 2 December 2010)

Most likely the growth of new social networking sites and opportunities also contributed to the fizzling out of Sister SF. Similar to the fate of the Sisterdjs mailing list, once social networking sites became popular such tight-knit collectives may no longer have seemed necessary (Wellman 2001). With the range of social media technologies now available, individuals have the capacity to establish and maintain their own loosely bounded networks, unconstrained by such limiting elements as geographical locale or web content managers (Baym 2007).

Conclusion

The efforts of collectives like Sister SF have begun to make possible events that highlight women EDM DJs, like the one described in the opening of this chapter. In many respects Sister SF's dedication to building and cultivating an alternative space for women in EDM both online and offline reflects characteristics of feminist and DIY collectives. Despite Sister SF's aversion to the word 'feminism', the collective's actions are representative of feminist goals and interests.

According to organizational communication scholars (Martin 1990), there is no consensus regarding what qualities constitute an organization as 'feminist'. Liberal feminists in particular do not consider hierarchical structures like those Sister SF adopted to be necessarily anti-feminist (Ferree 1988, as cited in Martin 1990). The group also valued non-competitive and inclusive altruistic practices, such as sharing DJ resources and providing networking opportunities for women DJs. Specific branding, management and internship strategies were in place to ensure consistency and a high degree of professionalism. They were also the collective's means of maintaining control over Sister's image and politics, especially as new chapters were added to its network.

The collective is an instructive case study because of the corporate/commercial practices it embraced and implemented to further feminist goals. As Chapter 3 also demonstrated, it is rare for women-centred cottage industries or music communities to employ branding strategies and a system of centralized, hierarchical control. This study suggests that these practices can be implemented successfully to promote a feminist agenda – whether or not it is labelled as such – and move women from the margins to the centre of spaces in which they historically have had little power. As members of Sister note, such progress has finally begun in San Francisco and New York City.

Despite the proliferation of social media tools and the success of some female DJs, the slow inroads women have made into production illustrate the existence of a much wider gender gap in EDM producing than in DJing. Many women – including several Sister residents – expressed an interest in becoming producers. Yet the reality is that few women complete tracks and even fewer secure distribution on recognized EDM labels. Chapter 5 expands upon the gender–technology connection discussed in Chapter 1 along with the themes of identity and community addressed throughout this book to focus on women's experiences with the production side of EDM culture.

Notes

1. The term 'residents' is commonly used in DJ culture to refer to members of a particular collective or other EDM entities such as clubs or production companies.

2. Male DJs are only invited to participate in Sister SF's annual event called 'Dragnet – We Like Boys', at which they must perform in drag. 2006 marked the ninth annual Dragnet event (www.sistersf.com).

3. In this context, the term 'distros' refers to independent online distribution services that specialize in selling girl-made 'zines.

4. The original Sister NYC website was still available online at www.sisterusa.com as of 11 June 2008.

Chapter 5

Producing Producers: Exploring Women's Place in
the Production of Electronic Dance Music

In the mid-2000s, Ashley Adams, who sometimes referred to her music-producing self as Seeress, lived in San Francisco's famous Haight-Ashbury district – now overrun with commercial chain stores. She lived a life fairly typical of twenty-something artists in the city, renting a room in a large Victorian house with six roommates. To support herself and her music-making interests she worked two part-time jobs, as a nanny and in the office of an up-and-coming local band. Ashley spent most of her time off reading manuals and teaching herself how to use the production gear she had either purchased or acquired on loan from a few acquaintances. On occasion she ventured out into San Francisco's bustling night life to listen to a DJ or producer.

I visited Ashley on a cool, grey Thursday evening in May 2005. We had hung out earlier in the month and before that in 2003 but this was the first time that we met at the house that she temporarily called home. After two bus rides and a short walk I approached the house and rang the doorbell. Ashley greeted me at the door and led me through a long hallway into the kitchen and down the stairs to the basement, where all of her belongings, including her music-making gear, were stored in the single room she called home. Inspirational messages – some cut out of magazines and newspapers, others handwritten – adorned the walls, giving some sense of comfort to the disheveled space. For the next couple of hours I sat on the futon couch that doubled as Ashley's bed, while she related stories about what it was like to be a young woman with a passion for making electronic music in a city where she had so few EDM connections.

Unlike most of the other women interviewed for this project, Ashley was not a DJ. She had no interest in collecting and playing other people's music; rather, she focused solely on creating music of her own. Her situation is rare for a number of reasons. The strong presence of female DJs in the city generally encourages women to pursue DJing before they adopt an interest in producing. In addition, the proliferation of dance clubs in the city provides an incentive for women with a keen interest in EDM to pursue DJing as an extra source of income.

Several of Ashley's stories related the challenges she faced as a struggling EDM artist – challenges she believed were exacerbated by being a woman. She recounted a particularly disappointing experience with the man running the sound at one of her live performances:

I was setting up my equipment and I disappeared for a minute. The band had taken my power strip and started plugging their stuff into it. The sound guy took it and gave it to the band, but I was going on before the band. [It] threw off my whole vibe. I'm a firm believer in making friends with the sound guy 'cause they make you or break you. Having the power strip stolen was a huge symbol of disrespect to me 'cause if I was a guy, and I hate saying this, I hate bringing in this if-I-was–a-guy statement, but it's true. If I was a guy setting up all my gear and I went to go to the bathroom and came back I doubt he would have stolen my power strip, you know.

(7 May 2005 interview)

Ashley's experience illustrates the gender and power dynamics at play in making and performing music. As the research on women and rock attests, her experiences are not unique to women in EDM specifically. Numerous women who work with sound technologies in EDM or more experimental or avant-garde music feel that their experiences in these scenes are unique because they are women (Rodgers 2010).

The distinctive qualities and practices associated with making EDM continue to situate most women outside of its production. Because women's engagement in EDM production is still in its infancy, this chapter is concerned primarily with the obstacles women face in their efforts to produce EDM. In addition, to illustrate the openings that are enabling women to progress in their production efforts, it also highlights a few success stories of women who have completed and distributed EDM tracks.

In this chapter I expand on significant obstructions including industry and studio politics, limited financial resources, gender socialization practices and access to gear and social networks. Some key openings I address include collaboration practices, formal education at higher learning institutions and digital distribution outlets. Contrasting women's divergent experiences and outcomes results in a deeper understanding of the environments and circumstances in which women can flourish as EDM producers.

Figure 5.1: Ashley Adams working with production gear, Berkeley, CA (2005).

DJing versus producing

Although this project is mainly concerned with DJs, this chapter focuses on producing because many DJs believe the next step in distinguishing themselves from other DJs and gaining status within EDM culture is to acquire the skills to produce music; most of them already have the desire. The connection between DJing and producing is logical, especially given the actions and qualities on which the EDM DJ's skills are evaluated. By combining what seem at times complementary and at times disparate tracks to create a seamless mix in which tracks are sped up, slowed down, subjected to equalizing effects and otherwise altered, the EDM DJ becomes a producer in her own right.

One of the first EDM DJs to popularize the idea of the DJ as composer in the 1990s was Jeff Mills. A Detroit native whose reputation developed while he was living in Chicago, he describes the ultra-minimal tracks he released on his Purpose Maker label as 'DJ tools'. In other words, they were purposefully unfinished and only ever became temporarily complete when mixed with other tracks. Music critic and scholar Simon Reynolds refers to these tracks as 'DJ food, the raw ingredients for cut 'n' mix' (1999: 281). In their history of the disc jockey, Brewster and Broughton (2000) summarize the move from DJ to producer, noting:

> Most successful DJs now carry the job title DJ/producer/remixer. Making their own records, or reconstructing those made by others, is a natural extension of the club DJ's trade, a way to put his creative stamp on the world. It's a way of distilling the particular sound he favors in his club performances into a more tangible form and, importantly, it's how a DJ can most convincingly claim artist status.
>
> (352)

While producing is a way to cement one's visibility in EDM culture, the experiences of the women interviewed rarely reflect Brewster and Broughton's characterization of the transition from DJ to producer as a 'natural' or effortless extension. Based on their interviews with male DJs-turned-producers, the authors conclude that 'most DJs would agree that the leap from playing records to making them is a small one; few see the move from DJ booth to recording studio as anything other than a natural progression' (353). Contrary to Brewster and Broughton's findings, the experiences presented here suggest that the leap from DJ to producer – from consuming and mixing records to producing and distributing them – can be quite challenging, especially for women.

Until the 2000s, when the availability of EDM increased initially through CDs and subsequently through digital downloads, the primary means of acquiring it was to frequent specialty record stores that sold tracks predominantly as 12-inch singles on vinyl. To mix tracks – whether on vinyl, on CD or as MP3s – a DJ must have access to the necessary equipment. At minimum, a DJ setup at this time consisted of two turntables (or CD mixers), a mixer, headphones, an amplifier and speakers. To accommodate digital downloads, additional MP3 mixing software was also becoming popular. This was a transitional time in that most of the DJs interviewed were still DJing with vinyl, but a few had moved on to CDs. The practice of DJing solely with iPods and/or DJ applications on iPhones had not yet begun.

The producer's role is to create the tracks that DJs buy. Until the digital revolution of the 2000s, the process of producing EDM from start to finish was arduous. It involved creating tracks to be sent to the appropriate record labels, in an effort to find one that would commit to pressing the tracks and distributing them to suitable retailers. Once on the retailer's shelf, they would sit in bins in the form of 12-inch vinyl, where producers hoped desperately they would catch a DJ's or aficionado's eye.

Unlike DJs, whose days involve a great deal of PR work to stay in the public's consciousness, producers usually have the luxury of a more low-key lifestyle. Their tracks themselves, through distribution and circulation, act as PR material in lieu of personal appearances. Thus, their craft is a much less social one than DJing. Many producers spend most of their time working alone in studios.

When asked about her process, Chantal Passamonte, who has released several albums with the independent label Warp under the moniker Mira Calix, explained, 'Although I'm quite sociable, I need to counteract that with being alone a lot. So actually for me it feels quite comfortable, 'cause I enjoy solitude. I don't ever feel particularly lonely' (Rodgers 2010: 131). For some women, this key difference between the social nature of DJing and the solitary practice of producing is reason enough for their resistance to production, despite their understanding of its potential career benefits. Forest Green [Melissa Green] explains how the need to self-promote affects her interest in producing:

> My job as a DJ is 80% being out, talking to people, promoting events. 20% of it or less is buying records and practicing. The rest is all promotion, being in people's face. Producing, most of the producers I know, I don't see them out that much. Unless they're playing, they're probably out producing because it takes a lot of time and that's a little scary for me. You stop going out and all of a sudden people forget about you.
>
> (7 July 2003 interview)

In some ways this situation is not unique to women. Both men and women who DJ encounter a great deal of competition and need to constantly be out in public promoting themselves. However, men's greater access to EDM networks and subcultural capital creates an environment in which it is even more critical for women to maintain and promote their public visibility. Yet Forest's desire to make music despite her hesitations and conflicts represents the mindset of most of the women interviewed. In sum, the move from DJing to producing can be difficult, especially for women who are marginalized in the politicized spaces of the record industry and recording studios.

Industry and studio politics

The current situation of women in EDM is similar to that of other popular music genres such as punk (Reddington 2003), hip hop (Rose 1994; Guevara 1996; Pough 2004) and indie rock (Kruse 2003; Leonard 2007). In her history of hip hop, Tricia Rose (1994) argues that women were not encouraged to contribute to the production of hip hop culture in the Bronx in the 1970s, and when they chose to do so, the efforts of female breakdancers, graffiti artists and rappers were often overlooked. Similarly, Helen Reddington (2007) argues that female instrumentalists have been written out of the history of punk in England, despite the presence of numerous female musicians in bands at the time of punk's formation.

In *Site and Sound: Understanding Independent Music Scenes*, Holly Kruse (2003) writes at length about women's involvement in independent record labels and the problems female artists encounter at the distribution level. Similarly, Marion Leonard (2007) is concerned with how female rock performers negotiate the gendering of rock as masculine. Other critics have addressed gender differences in terms of the consumption of popular music (Thornton 1996; Straw 1997). As Kruse (2003) notes, 'the gendered power relations of mainstream music production and consumption were to a large degree reproduced in indie music culture' (138), a genre that critics associate with local or trans-local scenes or culture, independent record labels and a diverse range of musical influences from punk to electronica (Kruse 1993, 2003; Leonard 2007).

An understanding of the gender relations to which Kruse (2003), Leonard (2007) and others refer requires some knowledge of the politics of both the music industry and the recording and production studio. Following the lead of Marion Leonard (2007), the term 'music industry' is used here to refer to a broad range of institutions and individuals including record companies, studios, musicians, producers and staff. Both major and independent record labels – whose interdependence is critical to the industry's modes of operation – are considered to be part of the business (Negus 1992; Hull 2004).

In recent years much discussion has focused on the recording industry's oligopolistic state and gatekeeping processes, and their impact on the kinds of artists who secure record deals, the artistic process of making music and the goals of record companies, which are increasingly concerned with their financial portfolios (Negus 1998, 1999; McLeod 2002; Hull 2004). In *Producing Pop*, Keith Negus (1992) suggests that 'the boundary between the recording industry and potential artists is not so much a gate where aspiring stars must wait to be selected and admitted, but a web of relationships stretched across a shifting soundtrack of musical, verbal and visual information' (46). Negus (1999) further argues that the broader cultural patterns within which a company is situated influence how these relationships work. Pertinent to this argument is his statement that 'the "intuitive" assumptions that staff make when acquiring the most suitable new artists and pieces of music are based on beliefs informed by a series of gender, class and racialized divisions' (21).

Researchers who have examined the gendered divisions within the dance music industry thus far have noted that most DJs and producers are men (Reynolds 1999; Fikentscher 2000), and that the same is true of other powerful industry positions such as label owners or club managers. As early as 1988, Angela McRobbie observed that upper management and other key decision-making jobs were dominated by an 'old boys' network' or 'boys' club'. Writing on EDM a few years later she added:

[I]t is still much easier for girls to develop skills in those fields which are less contested by men than it is in those already occupied by them. Selling clothes, stage-managing at concerts, handing out publicity leaflets, or simply looking the part, are spheres in which a female presence somehow seems natural.

(1994: 145)

These observations echo the situation in the broader popular music industry (Negus 1992), including, surprisingly perhaps, the findings of indie rock scholars (Kruse 1993, 2003; Leonard 2007). In Kruse's words, 'nothing about the social and economic organization of alternative music necessarily seeks to subvert the white, patriarchal structures of the mainstream music establishment' (1993: 40). As a genre, indie rock embodies a DIY philosophy and the popular understanding is that it is more open to female participation than other forms of rock because it is not associated with an overtly masculine agenda. Yet Leonard's extensive study is one of the latest to argue that the genre is still 'produced as a *gendered culture* that affects those who work within it' (2007: 4; italics in original).

Leonard's (2007) research is based on a decade of participating in and observing the ways in which gendered notions of rock music and the culture of the music industry are maintained and reproduced. A recent report on female DJs and sound engineers in the United Kingdom, for example, concluded that while 5–15 per cent of working DJs are women, the figure is much smaller for female sound engineers, who comprise only 2–5 per cent of their profession, mostly concentrated in live sound engineering (Smail, cited in Leonard 2007: 52). Research on the music industry and production studios offers some suggestions as to why this might be the case. Historically, the studio environment has been constructed as a male space that exudes an 'all lads together camaraderie' generally not available to women, whose place in the music industry came to be limited to the press department (Steward and Garrett, cited in Negus 1992).

Louise Meintjes' (1993) comprehensive ethnographic work on the politics of Zulu music production in the South African music industry in the early 1990s offers insight into how and why the studio space is a tightly guarded territory. Meintjes describes the studio space as a magical, fetishized space consisting of complex interiors, including 'the internal workings of electronic machines, the components of sounds, and the interiority of the artist', which together enhance the aura of the studio (98). At one point during Meintjes' fieldwork a studio engineer contemplates excluding her from a recording session to preserve both the creative process and the studio's aura, and so as not to demystify its symbolic value and the engineer's compositional processes. Meintjes notes that the 'magician-like status of the studio's technicians increases concomitantly with the expansion of the aura of the studio and its technology' (101). In other words, from a producer's perspective, allowing outsiders access to this male-centred technological environment would demystify the production process and potentially lower the symbolic and/or use value of the studio space.

Social boundaries rooted in technical knowledge and language also exacerbate studio labour divisions (Porcello 1991). Although Porcello's research is concerned primarily with the shift from formal student/apprentice to professional sound engineer, his analysis of conversations between producers and students in sound recording studios suggests additional factors that can discourage women from engaging in the studio space or employing a range of technologies for music-making purposes. In his study, Porcello analyses conversations between producers and students who are part of a sound-recording technology programme at a public Texas university. He argues that the success of these programmes is determined by how well students can reproduce the complex technical discourse of the field – full of metaphors, industry terminology and abbreviations – because the competency of sound engineers is measured based on their ability to engage this discourse. Given that most women do not show an interest in EDM beyond the dance floor until they are in their 20s or 30s, the college programme route is not an option for most of them.

Porcello also points out that to be admitted to the programme, applicants must be accepted as regular students in music school, a process that requires performance auditions and some knowledge of music theory. Historically, academia has not been a significant route into EDM production. Similar to hip hop artists, many EDM DJs and producers have little or no formal musical training. Given the informal environments in which 'tricks of the trade' and the associated technical discourse are shared in EDM culture, these can be especially difficult for women to access.

Despite these obstacles, some women are motivated to explore producing because of what DJ XJS [Annie Shaw] and others I interviewed referred to as a 'frustrating lack' of tracks produced by women. These women were aware that in the uncertain and sometimes disorganized economic world of independent labels, it is not unusual for producers to be paid poorly or not at all for their production efforts. Nevertheless, their actions were motivated in part by goodwill and a desire to get women on the EDM map as producers.

However, labels have the power to determine whether or not an artist is signed. Since the days of disco, major record labels have formed specialized dance divisions in an effort to attract musicians and staff with the credibility and subcultural knowledge so valued in dance music culture. Although the relations between the majors and independents vary from one label to the next, it is significant that a lot of dance music is released on labels with ties to the majors that honour the traditional, socially constructed gender roles discussed above. In most cases, label managers, owners, executives and artists and repertoire representatives are men, while women continue to be ghettoized as PR personnel.

In the 2000s Tyler Stone, one of the few female producers interviewed, was having a difficult time forging connections with independent labels despite having some success with this process in the early 1990s. In part, she attributes her experience to the increased homogenization of EDM since the 1990s. As its popularity grew it became more conservative, with white, heterosexual men becoming its key players. This was very different from its early days, in which African American and Latino men, a large number of whom were gay, dominated the scene (Fikentscher 2000).

As the cultural environment changed and the scene's structure came to more closely resemble that of the mainstream popular music industry, it became even harder to find female producers. As Tyler Stone notes:

> I was [the only woman producer] for at least a couple years and it was a different scene back then. Way less hetero, way more gay, much easier to be a woman. It got harder and harder. So I went from going to the World Music Conference and being able to go, 'Hey girl' and do that whole thing, to being asked, 'Whose girlfriend are you?'
>
> (17 May 2005 interview)

In other words, Stone felt that her insider status and ability to converse on a level playing field with other EDM artists who attend the renown annual World Music Conference in Miami Florida dissipated as EDM's popularity grew. Working outside the confines of EDM in what she calls 'the arts community', sound artist and electronic musician Jessica Rylan echoes Tyler Stone's observations about the changes within and beyond electronic music spaces. In her words, 'when I look at mainstream culture now from a feminist consciousness, I think things were better for women in the '80s or '90s. It was certainly a lot less exploitative than it is now' (Rodgers 2010: 146–147).

In summary, music industry and recording studio politics continue to reproduce gendered power relations that marginalize women, limiting their ability to produce EDM. In the next section I present a more detailed discussion of the social qualities of DJing compared to those of producing, then move on to identify some of the most prominent psychological and material hurdles that aspiring female producers must overcome.

The social qualities of DJing

Most of the women interviewed express a desire to heighten their artistic profile in EDM culture. In an effort to increase their visibility it is common for them to learn how to build websites in order to announce their gigs and post their DJ sets. Having an online presence can increase a DJ's likelihood of obtaining bookings at clubs and other events that can lead to more fame. Industry personnel push the notion that to become well known, DJs must move into production. Thus, despite the difficulties they experience in their production efforts, it is common for women to still refer to the move from DJ to producer as a 'natural' next step that is necessary to pursue in order to distinguish themselves from other DJs and in turn advance their careers.

In 2003, DJ Amber was a full-time DJ with an interest in learning how to produce tracks. Most DJs at the time were experiencing difficulties in the economically depressed dot-com bust era. Yet also at this time, one music-related booking agency was attempting to specialize in a roster of female clientele. DJ Amber was one of the women approached by the agency.

> I was like, 'Oh, I get it.' He's like, 'I can't market you if you don't have any tracks.' I was like, 'I'll have a track for you.' He was like push, push, push. You get marketed around just having a track, then if it's a hit, people are buying it. Then they'll book you to come play. It's just something you have to do. [I] think I'll love it once I get over the technical hurdle.
>
> (16 July 2003 interview)

As Amber's experience demonstrates, powerful industry personnel also promote the idea that the move from DJing to producing is both logical and natural. This point is echoed by Tammy Anderson (2009), whose analysis of contemporary rave culture highlights the increasing pressure on DJs to produce original material to advance and establish themselves.

Nevertheless, when they did experiment with producing, many women found the process to be quite isolating in ways they did not enjoy. In 2004 DJ Amber worked on a remix for the local independent band Karmacoda, collaborating with an experienced producer she met while teaching classes at a DJ Academy in San Francisco. In 2008 she produced another remix for the band, this time on her own. Amber's dedication and motivation were central to her ability to complete the track. In her words, 'It was just being totally tenacious with a piece of software that was intuitive to me – I used [Sony] ACID [Pro] – it was all self-taught.'

However, despite her initial determination to produce and her ability to complete a remix on her own, Amber decided against pursuing producing further. 'I stepped away from production because it's too isolating. Music and production for me has always been about other people. Sharing it with other great people who have become close friends. I enjoy that a lot' (5 January 2011 personal communication). In 2008 she decided to join a band as a vocalist in addition to maintaining her DJ activity.

Several other women also related their love of DJing to its social aspects, such as meeting new people and interacting with a crowd. As Samira [Samira Vijghen] explains:

> For me, it's like the oral tradition where you have that immediate call and response. A lot of the way your story is told is being dictated by your audience. The nature of it is changing as a result of the audience that is immediately there, and I really like that about spinning. It's pretty much the only thing I do in my life that I do straight from the gut. I never plan my sets no matter how much I try. My CDs are very different from my live sets. I like to collaborate with people.
>
> (20 May 2005 interview)

Like DJ Amber and Samira, a number of the other women interviewed emphasized the centrality of social interaction to their enjoyment of the DJ role, noting that they considered themselves more social than many of their male counterparts. Unlike male DJs, whom the women often viewed as having a cool and static presence behind the turntables, these women felt they interacted more with their audiences via visual cues like eye contact and dancing. Thus, the value and enjoyment they attribute to the social qualities of DJing constitute internal factors that may prevent women from pursuing production. In the next section I examine external factors that also hinder women from becoming producers, including production costs, a lack of collaborative opportunities and barriers to knowledge acquisition.

Production costs, limited opportunities and barriers to knowledge

With a few exceptions, the women I interviewed were in their 20s and 30s. Having reached adulthood, many had family and work responsibilities. The situation of women in EDM in the 2000s mirrored that of women in rock bands in the 1990s. In her study of skill acquisition in rock bands, Mary Ann Clawson (1999) found that 87.5 per cent of the men (21 of 24) compared to 26 per cent of the women (5 of 19) had joined their first bands before high school graduation. Almost half (47 per cent) of the women in her study did not join bands until they were past college age, at which time they had significant catching up to do and little leisure time in which to do it. Clawson attributes the difference between when men and women join their first band to the masculinity that is inherent in rock bands. She notes that during adolescence rock bands function as sites of masculinity that conflate music and masculinity. They also derive their personnel from peer groups. In turn, their composition mirrors the sex-segregated organization of pre-teen and early adolescent social life.

As with rock bands, much EDM pedagogy takes place informally via one's social network. Given the age at which most women begin DJing and the fact that so few of them are 'superstar DJs', it is necessary for them to work other jobs in addition to DJing, which leaves them little time to devote to their EDM interests compared to some men. As DJ KT [Katie Pollard] explained:

Of the DJs I know, the women tend to have more stuff going on in their lives besides just being a DJ, like being a student, having a demanding job or having a family. A lot of guys do too, but there are also a bunch of guys I know, and these are the ones who are writing music, who don't have much else to do besides music all the time. They either have a job that's not really demanding or they don't have a job at all. I don't know why there are more guys in that category and more of the women I know are out doing other stuff, but that seems to be the case.

(18 June 2005 interview)

In addition to DJ KT, who is a statistician, several other women also had full-time jobs that required them to work with computers. As a result, many expressed a lack of desire to spend their evenings and weekends on the computer learning to use music-making software.

As DJ KT notes, in addition to the ways in which work responsibilities impacts women's time and desire to produce EDM, familial responsibilities – which often increase as women age – also affect their production success. Detroit-based DJ Minx [Jennifer Witcher] was the only EDM artist I interviewed who was also a mother. When we met in 2003 she had two young children and had been a very active DJ, regularly playing at clubs in Detroit and elsewhere, since the early 1990s. After a decade of DJing, DJ Minx became interested in producing and started her own label, Women on Wax. She was fortunate enough to be able to stay at home with her youngest daughter while she worked on her EDM career.

> I have a studio in my home so it's really easy to work. I have a one year old and I gotta take care of my girls. [My husband] suggested I could stay home, take care of the girls and run my label. If I have a small tour for like 10 days he'll take care of the girls, but I work my butt off so there's not much for him to do [while I'm gone].
>
> (13 August 2003 interview)

Even with the full support of a husband, DJing regularly – sometimes internationally – and running a record label while taking care of a family is a challenging balancing act that requires tremendous effort. Yet by 2010, Women on Wax had produced 15 releases.

For others, there are financial obligations that make moving into production an extremely difficult venture to pursue. In theory, the widespread availability of home computers and music production software democratized the EDM production process. Before the explosion of PCs, producing this music required access to analog equipment such as synthesizers, drum machines and samplers, so building a home studio could be extremely costly. Since the 2000s, however, anyone with a personal computer and the right software could become an EDM producer – or so the myth goes. In reality, learning to use music-making software can be difficult and while the trend towards all-digital studios continues, it is still most common for producers – including women – to work with both analog and digital gear (Rodgers 2010).

Consequently, production gear is still a costly and potentially risky investment even in the digital age. While a bedroom DJ setup is likely to cost upwards of $1000, a production studio's equipment needs can be much greater and more expensive. Tweakheadz lab, which claims to be 'the best site for learning music production', advertises components for a 'low cost' studio set-up at over $1100, in addition to the cost of a personal computer. The 'Mac dream studio' components total $12,000.

In addition to the initial equipment costs, DJs need to continually purchase fresh, original tracks to acquire bookings at clubs and EDM events. While a decent number of the women interviewed regularly secured paid gigs, few were able to live off those earnings. Most women invest their time and money in their DJ practices because of their love of the art of DJing, not because it necessarily leads to financial rewards. On average, the women interviewed spent $100–$150 a month on music, although it is not unusual for individuals to spend much more. During her first six months of DJing, DJ Barbarella [Barbara Mayers] spent $300 a week on records. In 2005, she owned $20,000 worth of vinyl.

As a teenager, DJ Blondie [Ilana Pearlman], who was 18 years old when we first met and the youngest woman interviewed, babysat to earn money to buy records:

> I always thought to myself: two hours of babysitting is one record. I started thinking of everything in my life in terms of how much a record would cost. Oh I shouldn't buy that shirt – that's three records. It was really funny. It gets really expensive, $10 a record ends up being $12 a record with tax, times all my records. That ends up being a lot of money.
>
> (19 June 2003 interview)

For many women like DJ Blondie, saving money to purchase music can be difficult. The fact that women in most occupations, music-related or otherwise, are paid less than men even when they are doing the same work exacerbates the situation. Moreover, the money spent on DJ tools like records – which were more costly than MP3s – often left little remaining for production equipment.

In a 2005 interview, Forest Green highlighted knowledge acquisition and financial investment, in addition to her PR responsibilities, as the reasons she had not yet made a serious effort to produce music.

> It's the long hard road, yet one that I've chosen, but I'm hoping that my computer background in video production will help me with music production. I have lots of friends who are producers and have their own labels. It's not like starting from ground zero. I want to build my own studio and have it be mine, like all the other women producers that I know who have their own studios, and I respect that. A whole other level of money – spending to get all your gear and then there's a whole other level of learning all about gear and technology.
>
> (9 May 2005 interview)

Next, I turn to a larger discussion of the benefits of collaboration that include confidence building and access to insider knowledge.

Confidence

In terms of technology, the DJs interviewed were comfortable using not only DJ-specific technologies such as turntables and mixers, but also computer technology. Nevertheless, many of them had little confidence in their ability to engage in the production process.

DJ Amber's situation, discussed above, is fairly representative of my findings. Her interest in teaching DJ classes but not producing music puts her in the category of many women whose work involves helping others or requires strong interpersonal skills, but does not involve them in the more technical aspects of the field. This division is exemplified by the PR departments that have come to represent women's primary place in the music industry (Negus 1992; Kruse 2003).

The gender stratification women experience in work-related settings limits their opportunities and in turn their confidence in working with technology in other settings. Women spoke at length about using their interpersonal skills to develop favourable reputations in the scene, but few felt comfortable pursuing interests that required them to learn new technical skills. When she was initially interested in learning how to make music, DJ Amber explained:

> I was not the person at my house pulling apart transistor radios and building little circuit boards – that was my brother and I didn't even ask him what he was doing. I didn't know and I didn't care. My brother's work made funny noises. I thought that was cool and that was about it. Women are less prone to be that sort of tinkering-minded; they're not the ones who program the clocks on the VCR. I hate to generalize but it's the truth.

(16 July 2003 interview)

The stereotype of women as technically inept is reinforced throughout popular culture, and girls receive this message long before reaching adulthood. Those who take an interest in EDM as adults are still subjected to the message that experimenting with technology and making music is men's work. For example, music magazines in general – not only those that focus on EDM or production gear – continue to be filed under the Men's Interest sections at major bookstores, and advertisements in EDM magazines such as *Remix* and *XLR8R* overwhelmingly feature men in ads for drum machines and music composition software.

The perpetuation of discourses and practices that situate women on the margins of technology produces a culture in which they have limited exposure and opportunities to contribute to technology-centred environments, both within and beyond the music industry.[1] As discussed in Chapter 1, feminist and cultural studies scholars agree that technology is not neutral or inherently masculine; rather, conventions and social practice, along with popular narratives and economic relations, have shaped its uses (Oldenziel 1999; Wajcman 2004). More than two decades after Cynthia Cockburn observed that women 'may push the buttons but they may not meddle with the works' (1985: 12), her observation holds true for women in EDM. The progress women have made in producing lags far behind the advances they have made as DJs.

Yet even here there are exceptions, which are often accounted for by influential if non-traditional childhood experiences. Ashley Adams, the struggling producer whose story opened this chapter, traces her interest in producing to her early years, long before she was introduced to EDM:

> My mom and dad thought I was going to be an engineer because when I was little I was taking apart my radios and stuff. My producing all started with Liz [Wheeler] handing me a drum machine a year ago. It was almost intuitive. I figured it out on my own. I was making songs on it on my own. Now that I have all these crazy robots [analog gear] and I have to have a pep talk with myself before I sit down and I'm like, you're going to shift into your logical thinking brain and you're not going to be intimidated by this stuff because someone on this planet somewhere programmed it and made it. You know this is not out of your realm of accessibility.
>
> (23 June 2003 interview)

Ashley's relationship to technology is unique among the women I interviewed. Yet even she reported undergoing a constant psychological struggle with herself over her abilities, as even her confidence and previous experience tinkering with technology were not enough to bring her to producing. There was a necessary third element – a social intervention – that set her on her path. Only after interacting with a female DJ, whose boyfriend owned a drum machine, did she finally set out on a course to making music. Nevertheless, Ashley's opportunities in this arena remained limited because she lacked access to fellow producers and other powerful individuals in the local EDM scene.

Accessing insider knowledge

Despite the many social aspects of DJing highlighted by women DJs, they also noted that learning how to DJ itself was a solitary process. Their training or instruction rarely went beyond a brief 'how to' session, usually given by a male friend. Of course, even with little formal training, they had some knowledge of how to put a record on a turntable, a point of reference from everyday life from which to begin learning to 'play' with records. They had some direction from which to learn how to scratch, tweak and blend beats. This experiential knowledge is even more abundant in the age of the MP3.

Compared to DJing, producing music is a much less intuitive process; analog music production gear and high-end digital software offer few immediate cues as to how they work. Learning to produce involves acquiring 'techno speak' in a manner similar to learning a new language, and many women perceive the learning curve to be very steep. In a 2003 interview, DJ Amber articulated the hurdles she had been dealing with for the previous two years:

> I can write plenty of songs in my head, and I do all the time. But there's this logic gap where the software and intricacies of getting audio quality just right and balanced and all

this garbage. It's a huge hurdle, which has nothing to do with why I got into DJing, which is why I think you find so many DJs being non-producers. The one doesn't meld well with the other. You have to kinda walk yourself over there, roll your eyes, alright I gotta do it, but then I think: in fact I know I'll grow to love it, but for right now this stupid software is getting in my way of being creative.

(16 July 2003 interview)

Several of the women observed that the best way to learn to produce is to locate an experienced producer to work with. However, they reported having difficulty finding producers who were willing to share their knowledge and from whom they felt comfortable learning.

As discussed in Chapter 3, in many music scenes – as Simon Frith (1981), Sarah Thornton (1996) and others have found in their research – people gain access to 'insider' knowledge and get to be 'in the know' by networking and spending time in record stores, in clubs, in studios and online. With the exception of information on the Internet, the social spaces and conversations that may encourage women to produce are often off-limits to them. Writing about her experiences as a sound engineer, for instance, Boden Sandstrom (2000) noted that many men are unwilling to share the powerful role of controlling sound, limiting opportunities for women to receive hands-on training. Additionally, even in conversations that take place online, women may feel excluded when men are present.

Even the practices and relations carried out in everyday talk produce a gendered relationship between women and rock or pop music culture, and provide another reason for women's continued marginalization in music production (Kruse 2003). Research that examines teens' discussions about pop music shows that adolescent boys tend to discuss instruments and equipment, whereas girls of the same age tend to talk more about lyrics, whether a song is danceable and the stars themselves (Steward and Garratt, cited in Kruse 2003). The next section looks at how women are turning to formal education to fill the knowledge gap, as music production courses become more widely available in post-secondary education.

Formal education

A few of the women interviewed mentioned enrolling in community college classes as a route to improving their technical skills in areas such as web design and audio production; however, only one of them had an educational background in university music departments. As Porcello (1991) indicated in his study, this is most likely because gaining admission to such programmes requires applicants to be accepted as regular students in the music school. The story of Kate Simko, a successful EDM producer who graduated from a four-year music production programme, is highlighted below to address the challenges of gaining access to such educational opportunities as well as the potential benefits for those who manage to do so.

Chicago-based Kate Simko was not a DJ before becoming a producer. Fortunate to have found her passion for EDM when she was still a teenager, Simko pursued a degree in digital music production at Northwestern University in Evanston, Illinois, a path that would not have been possible without her extensive background in piano performance. She was the only woman among the handful of students enrolled in the programme. Simko explained the arduous application process as follows:

> I saw that they had a music technology program. I had to audition at the level of a piano major at Northwestern and it's one of the top three piano schools in the U.S. It took me a year just to prepare for the audition so I started taking classical piano again just to study for my audition. On top of that I had to study classical piano at the level of a freshman performance for one year. There were film students and really creative people who wanted to do stuff and they were like no, you have to be straight up virtuoso to study electronic music … That's where I was able to learn, to be nurtured and be given credit in school and have the time and the luxury to be getting credit through Northwestern to figure out how to make electronic music.
>
> (29 May 2008 interview)

A number of factors coalesced for Kate Simko to be able to pursue the production of EDM via this route, the most important being years of formal training and a talent in piano performance that most people do not have. Her discography includes numerous original tracks and remixes, several of which have been released by Spectral Sound, the companion label to Ghostly International. Ghostly International is an independent record label based in Ann Arbor, Michigan that has generated accolades from a range of music and media outlets worldwide, including *Rolling Stone*, *Billboard* and *Advertising Age*. Spectral Sound is dedicated to more dance-floor-oriented music, compared to the ethereal electronic sounds released on Ghostly. As of 2010, Simko was the only woman among the 21 artists featured on the label's roster. As the first and only woman signed to the prestigious label, Spectral Sound took the liberty of dubbing her the 'first lady of techno'. In the past few years a number of internationally respected EDM labels have released Simko's music and she continue to DJ and perform live all across the globe. Her case demonstrates the benefits of pursuing an intense educational path for gaining skills useful for EDM production, but it also illustrates how inaccessible such programmes remain for most aspiring producers.

It is also worth noting that high school music education programmes generally offer little instruction in electronic music production. In a study in the United Kingdom published in 2001, Sloboda found that the offerings in British schools seriously lag behind those available in non-school environments when it comes to technological resources and know-how. He concluded that classroom music instruction as currently conceptualized and organized is an inappropriate vehicle for mass music education in the twenty-first century.

Figure 5.2: Kate Simko performs at the Decibel Festival in Seattle, WA (2011). Photographer: Glenn Jackson.

Perhaps even more disappointing is the finding that even when music-making technology is introduced into the classroom, old social patterns are reproduced. Cooper's (2007) study found that while both boys and girls expressed confidence in their ability to use music-making software, boys were more emphatic in their confidence compared to girls, who expressed less interest. Consequently, a far greater number of boys than girls attended the optional Friday lunch hour 'music technology club', creating yet another male-dominated electronic music learning space. The girls' lack of interest in the technology can be attributed in part to the pervasiveness of popular discourses that continue to define technology as the domain of boys and men. Unfortunately, thus far formal education has had a minimal impact on reversing this perception. However, collaboration, when available, is one way that women are overcoming the limitations imposed by these gendered discourses.

The benefits of collaboration

Women's limited access to the vital social networks of male DJs, producers and label owners also restricts their ability to develop knowledge of and experience with EDM production gear. As such, they have to work harder than men to access vital social networks and some women do not have the time to dedicate to forming these connections because of their additional responsibilities. However, when they can manage to do so, collaborative opportunities have proven to greatly enhance women's production experiences.

A prominent full-time DJ in the Bay Area, DJ Denise [Denise Rees], spoke at length about the importance that collaborating on her earliest productions has had on her career. Her production efforts have furthered her DJ career and expanded both her fan base and income. Because of her DJ success, DJ Denise had access to local male producers. In 2003, she was already talking about the important role that her extensive EDM network would have on her ability to pursue making music.

> It's definitely a matter of if you know someone. Same thing with wanting to be a DJ, but it seems like there are so many DJs out there that it's probably a lot easier to find someone with turntables than to find someone with a studio and actual gear. So I think that might have a little influence on why not as many girls are making beats, but I mean there's no reason why. I'm really itching to do it just because there's stuff that I want to hear that I haven't heard yet and it's in my head and I want to get it out there, but I know that it's a lot harder to make something. What you're thinking is very hard to transcribe onto the gear that you have.
>
> (8 July 2003 interview)

Like other women, DJ Denise emphasizes the difficulty and skill level involved in making a track, the need for access to gear and the importance of having a mentor. Yet she also says there is no reason why women cannot make music. The contradictions in her comments are difficult to reconcile and speak to the post-feminist sensibility of contemporary western culture, examples of which are discussed throughout this book.

Denise's statement at first acts as evidence of the ways in which post-feminist discourses conceal the rigid gender order still in play. More importantly, though, her contradictory position as a woman who struggles against this order's norms while espousing a post-feminist proviso of women's independence from such norms demonstrates how this philosophy limits the very independence it claims for women. If there is truly no reason women cannot make music, then those who do not or cannot are reduced to independent (failed) agents, rather than being viewed as constrained by a broader system of gendered oppression.

Since our initial meeting in 2003, DJ Denise has produced numerous tracks that have been released by several record labels, including her own label Muzimo Music. Her experiences and success speak to the value of having access to such a strong network. In her words, 'I was able to pick other people's brains, ask questions [and] learn and exchange tips' (8 July 2003 personal communication). In particular, she has commented on the collaborative process she engaged in with her first music partner, Aleks. 'He would do the actual engineering of the song while I sat beside him and made comments and suggestions. He would teach me as we went along with each track'. Denise and Aleks completed the track 'Machines' in December 2003.

> Toward the end of 2004, I received help from two other producer friends of mine who passed on some software for producing (Cubase 2.0 and a slew of VSTs, which are

essentially computer-based synthesizers), and once I had the software set up on my computer, I started making electronic music on my own.

(13 November 2008 personal communication)

Denise produced her first solo project, the trance track 'Simple Reform', in January 2005 and established Mizumo Music that same year. To enhance her production skills Denise enrolled in music production classes at Diablo Valley College, where she earned a certificate in Recording Arts a year and a half later. Since January 2006, she has released over 70 original collaborative and solo tracks and remixes. As of December 2010, Mizumo Music had 75 releases featuring over 100 artists. Yet even though the label is female-owned it still has the typical roster of men, which reflects the scarcity of female EDM producers.

DJ Denise's experiences working with men were positive in part because she had already proven herself as an EDM DJ. Research demonstrates that women's confidence grows when men are removed from the scene (Cockburn 1985; Rose 1994; Baker 2008). In other words, they find the presence of other women more motivating than the presence of men. For DJ Blondie, the most significant reason for her reluctance to learn about music production was the fact that EDM producers were overwhelmingly male.

There's maybe two women producers out of the thousands of psy-[chedelic] trance producers. No one ever wants to show you how to do it; they just expect you to know. When you go over to a guy's house and they tell you they're going to teach you, they DJ the whole time, where a girl would be like, 'Yeah, cool, now let me hear you try it.' Guys always table hog[2] because they want to show off. So with the whole technology thing you're intimidated because everyone else is trying to show off, especially guys who are dominant, who are very aggressive, [and] want to be in the spotlight.

(19 June 2003 interview)

DJ Blondie's frustrations speak directly to the need for women-centred production collectives. Even though DJ collectives can now be found worldwide,[3] no comparable collectives exist to promote the efforts of female EDM producers and few women are part of existing male-centred collectives.

Artists and researchers have noted that the gains made by girls and women tend to occur in women-centred EDM spaces. Pamela Z, a San Francisco-based composer, performer and sound artist, who works with sampling technologies and live electronic processing, has commented on how much more positive women's experiences are when the learning environment is off-limits to men. Speaking about women's reactions to the workshops she runs, she says:

They were like, 'I've taken these classes and all the men gather around and they won't let you touch anything, or they make you feel stupid' ... The women I taught were so shocked that it could be taught in plain language, and they could understand it. And then I realized that there was a total need for that, to do something specifically for women.

(Rodgers 2010: 225)

Research on role modeling confirms the value that can be gained from women specific training. Furthermore, findings regarding same-sex role models illustrate the need for not only women-centred but also girl-centred EDM production spaces, because the presence of same-sex role models can greatly influence the types of activities and interests individuals choose as they get older. As role models for girls, female technology teachers in particular 'can more directly change attitudes for both girls and boys about careers for females in technological fields' (Fiore 1999).

With respect to music in the classroom, Louise Cooper's (2007) study – which involved teaching year nine students to make music using the software program Dance eJay – found that 87 per cent of girls were partial to composing music in groups as opposed to individually compared to only 64 per cent of boys. In summary, standard EDM production practices generally involve single artists working in isolation; however, girls and women would benefit from reconceptualizing the production process in innovative ways that include more collaboration.

The pursuits of the group called female:pressure, 'an international database of female djs, producers and visual artists – mostly related to the electronic music scene' (http://www. femalepressure.net), offer examples of what may be gained when women are encouraged to collaborate on artistic projects. Viennese DJ and producer Electric Indigo [Suzanne Kirchmayr] established female:pressure in 1998; a decade later its database consisted of 980 artists from 51 countries. In 2005, media artist/programmer Andrea Mayr, also based in Vienna, created the 'open:sounds' project 'as an online production platform for the female:pressure community to exchange sounds and remix each others' tracks' (http://www. femalepressure.net/opensounds.html). The work of all participating producers is made available to the entire membership for new productions and remixes under the terms of the Attribution-NonCommercial-ShareAlike Creative Commons license.

Open:sounds' first official project was a compilation CD of 16 tracks produced by Vienna-based artists in 2006. In 2008, open:sounds pursued a more ambitious project, releasing 'female:pressure dvd 1'. The renowned Berlin-based label Hardwax distributed limited hard copies of the project, for which 17 Viennese VJs and artists created videos to accompany 21 original tracks produced by women internationally. Vienna's Verein Stadtimpuls Wien (Vienna City Impulse Association), an association that grants funds for projects and activities that have a strong positive impact on the local cultural environment, sponsored both of these projects. Government funding opportunities for such projects is unfortunately almost non-existent in the United States, despite examples illustrating a successful alternative model that not only encourages women to produce EDM but also provides a distribution outlet for their efforts.

Although women-centred production collectives are few and far between, digital media tools and networks themselves present additional opportunities for women to find more public outlets for their music. MP3 technology and digital distribution networks are useful to all music producers, but they have become especially vital for women because of the gendered power dynamics in popular music spaces. DJ Denise spoke about the ways such tools have been instrumental to her success, offering an insightful description of a networking process that depends on a range of digital technologies.

I initially set up relationships with labels by good old fashioned guerrilla tactics. I went on Beatport.com, went to the genre of labels that I wanted to work with, copied down about 1,200 different label names, and started searching online (via Google) for contact names and emails. Granted, I only got about 500 of those contacts successfully, and I still have about 700 to go! When I first contacted some of these labels, usually by Myspace, I asked for their contact email and also mentioned that I was available for remix work. I was hired on the spot for about ten jobs simply by asking – again, however, based on royalty agreements (usually 50 per cent). Now, when I am shopping out an original track, I send an MP3 link to the track to this list of 500 labels, and without fail, I get at least ten to fifteen replies from labels that are interested in signing the track.

(13 November 2008 personal communication)

Music producers in general, and women producers in particular, can greatly benefit from a range of collaborative opportunities. Such opportunities include working with more experienced artists of either sex, although women's confidence tends to flourish in women-centred spaces. Thus, establishing production collectives specifically for women and using the Internet and digital distribution sites to publicly showcase women's work are key methods for expanding women's involvement in EDM production.

It is worth noting that just as there were no obvious differences between the DJ sets and subgenre interests of the women I interviewed and those of men, there is also nothing inherent in the sounds of the tracks produced by Kate Simko, DJ Denise and other women that distinguishes their music from men's EDM compositions. This stems in part from the fact that EDM tracks rarely feature vocals, and in accordance with standard EDM production practices, when they do include vocal tracks, artists do not necessarily feature their own voices.

Whether or not women have deliberately chosen not to create a distinct 'women's EDM', there are logical reasons to avoid doing so. These include a tendency to label popular music that sounds feminine – that is music that critics characterize as soft and light – as inauthentic and the fact that female artists' work at times is more harshly criticized than the efforts of male musicians. Examining conversations on the popular music listserv Rocklist, Robert Walser (2008) observed that in discussions about Alanis Morissette's album *Jagged Little Pill* participants raised doubts about her authenticity and felt that 'her self-centered, personal, angst-ridden persona gives her work "a commercial edge"' (241). As a counterpoint Walsh remarks that Bruce Springsteen is also introspective but does not garner such criticism. He further notes that, "It's difficult to avoid seeing Morissette's gender, and that of her fans, as being at fault" (242).

To mark one's music as 'women's music' thus disadvantages female producers on two fronts: it may result in harsher criticism as well as distancing potential male fans. The latter concern is especially significant for producers because EDM is largely consumed by DJs, the majority of whom are men. Again, while further research is needed to understand women's interest in and motives for producing the kinds of EDM they make, this discussion illustrates some potential consequences of creating EDM that is distinctly labeled as women's music.

Conclusion

Though my larger project began with an interest in female DJs, once fieldwork was underway persistent questions emerged about the relationship between DJing and production. These questions fueled this chapter's purpose: to understand the connections, similarities and differences between these two distinct yet overlapping EDM practices. The exploration began with the question of why so few women produce EDM and/or why women experience such difficulty in finding distribution outlets for their work. My findings suggest that a range of social, discursive and material practices coalesce to account for the lack of female producers and the underrepresentation of EDM created by women.

An investigation of women's relative absence from EDM production must begin with the recognition that the politics of both the music industry and the recording studio continue to favour men, who are viewed as the de facto normative figures and who occupy the most powerful positions in the industry. Within the dance music industry itself women are often ghettoized in PR work. Additionally, the technical demands and boys' club mentality of the studio make this space particularly difficult for women to access.

It is important to note that while they share some commonalities, DJing and producing are distinct undertakings. Several women cited their highly developed PR abilities – such as strong interpersonal skills and outgoing personalities – as reasons why they enjoy DJing and consider producing to be too isolating. Those who are interested in producing are faced with the expense of production tools and the need to devote time to acquiring production skills while also juggling family and work responsibilities. Collaboration with more experienced producers, and to a lesser extent formal education, are two ways women have started to overcome these challenges.

In addition, the growing use of digital tools and networks also offers promising possibilities. Several studies, including one investigating the computer attitudes of white, middle-class, suburban 11- and 12-year-olds on the southern coast of England (North and Noyles 2002), have found that girls (far more than boys) do not believe that computer use is unalterably linked to factors such as gender and mathematics background. A year-long study in the

United States that explored the meanings 250 middle-school students assigned to computers suggests even more potential for change. While neither boys nor girls mentioned using the computer for music production, girls seemed to be more open-minded regarding its capabilities. They defined computers as 'multi-use tools' and often described the computer by saying 'it's whatever you want it to be'. In comparison, boys tended to express a more narrow view of the technology, identifying computers as machines or toys that made things quicker and easier (Christie 2005).

As girls' and women's access to computers and music production software expands, the boundaries between studio and bedroom producers continue to dissolve. Artists today have the ability to create praiseworthy music without the assistance of record labels, whose sizeable budgets for studio time, marketing and distribution were previously essential. Presently, countless online forums, websites and magazines – most notably *Remix* – feature reviews, interviews and tutorials as part of their growing collections of information for electronic musicians.

Moreover, as the number and popularity of online social networking tools and music distribution sites such as Beatport continue to expand, so do the distribution opportunities. This is especially significant for women, as it enables them to bypass the traditional channel of getting signed to a record label, which typically requires gaining the approval of the men who run the labels. In all, the visibility of the production efforts of women like DJ Denise and Kate Simko speak to the changes that are underway, even while women remain a small minority in the ever-expanding world of EDM artists.

Notes

1. For instance, according to Wilson (2003), only 19 per cent of computer science students at the college level are female.
2. 'Table hog' refers to someone who dominates the turntables and the amount of time DJing.
3. In 2010, they include the Ladyfingers DJ collective in Melbourne, Australia (www.myspace. com/ladyfingersdjs) and the six-woman collective Twee Grrrls Club in Toyko, Japan (search. japantimes.co.jp/cgi-bin/fm20101001a2.html).

Conclusion: Are the Tables Turning?

As evidenced by the experiences of women in EDM, popular press outlets and my years of participant observation, there remains an assumption that generally it is men who are interested in DJing and producing EDM. A recent issue of the *San Francisco Chronicle* featured a cover story titled, 'Bay Area DJs Shatter Sexist Preconceptions' (10–16 April 2011). Although the article focuses on female hip hop DJs, it is similar to other magazine and newspaper articles published over the years that call attention to female DJs in a variety of musical genres, in an effort to dispel the myth that all DJs are men. The repetition of this theme across time and genres speaks to women's continued struggle for recognition in EDM and other musical cultures.

Consequently, the aim of this book has been to examine and raise awareness of how women have moved beyond the dance floor to become EDM DJs and producers in their own right. To this end, I set out to map the various ways in which women's experiences are distinct from those of men pursuing similar paths. The resulting study examined a variety of historical, discursive, material and social practices both within and beyond EDM culture that account for these differences and explored how women have dealt with them.

One of the primary factors that shaped women's relationship to EDM was the reconfiguration of the term *technology*, which, as Chapter 1 explains, was redefined in the early twentieth century to refer to the expertise of men in science and engineering. This change introduced and ultimately naturalized the belief that men possess innate traits that predispose them to be the inventors of technology, whereas women's natural inclinations limit them to passively using the technology created by men. Over time, framing women as passive users has distanced them – both figuratively and literally – from audio and music technologies. The stereotype of women as inherently less interested in complex audio technologies fosters a belief that they are equally disinterested in learning about and collecting music.

Collectively, these conditions have significantly shaped the power dynamics of music subcultures and the music industry itself. In both types of spaces it is common for women's contributions to be overlooked or undervalued in comparison to those of men. Nevertheless, since the early days of amateur radio, there have always been some women who resisted such marginalization and pursued technology and music-based interests despite the obstacles they faced.

Moreover, the gender inequalities and gendered power dynamics that continue to shape western culture at large inevitably impact EDM culture as well. Popular culture generally and EDM environments specifically remain male-centric spaces in which women continue to be positioned and viewed as sex objects. In the brand-obsessed world of the twenty-first century, where distinctions between celebrity and DJ are disappearing, female DJs are forced to deal with a complex set of issues related to identity and representation. Chapter 2 highlighted the ways in which sexuality continues to play a prime role in the choices women make about their stage personas, in how they see themselves and in how others view them. Despite a desire to maintain their individuality, female DJs still formulate identities that fall within a pre-established range of acceptability.

Chapters 3 and 4 dealt with the strategies women have adopted to connect with other female DJs in their efforts to overcome a range of obstacles they confront in EDM culture, including isolation, marginalization and/or sexism, inexperience and lack of access to insider knowledge. Women's recognition of what can be gained from using technology speaks to their defiance of gendered assumptions about technology. Additionally, their creation of women-centred web spaces reflects their recognition of the power of the Internet and its potential for forging connections with other EDM artists across geographical spaces. In particular, the creation of websites, listservs and e-zines, along with the monthly potlucks in Portland, have been instrumental to women's acquisition of crucial social and subcultural capital.

Moving beyond DJing, Chapter 5 examined how the distinctive qualities and practices associated with EDM production continue to situate most women outside its boundaries. Although they can be complementary, the social skills required for effective DJing are markedly different from the qualities required for success in the production process, which many women viewed to be isolating and arduous. Nonetheless, the chapter ends on a hopeful note with the experiences of women who have made significant inroads in this area. Here again, digital networks and tools have proven extremely useful for bypassing gatekeeping practices that stem from industry and recording studio politics.

Throughout this work I have included the voices of as many of the women interviewed as possible, so that their stories, experiences and viewpoints would be conveyed in their own words. My participants' relationship to feminism was varied and complex, as it was on the radar of some and not of others. I have not attempted to speak for these women or make judgements about whether or not they are feminists; rather, I have drawn on feminist theory and writings about post-feminism as tools to contextualize the interviews and identify moments of feminism in action.

The reluctance on the part of many women to identify as feminists does, however, illustrate the success of post-feminist rhetoric. The danger here is that in distancing women from feminism, post-feminism creates an environment in which girls and women view their problems as individual rather than systemic, and hence may fail to see the connection between their own struggles, the struggles of others and the gendered power dynamics that govern their experience. Thus, one of my goals has been to narrow the gap between female EDM artists and feminism so that women in EDM as well as in other male-centric spaces recognize the systemic nature of the power disparities between men and women that structure these fields of interest. In doing so, I hope that they will be encouraged to continue their efforts during even the most trying times.

To provide a point of comparison, a potential direction for future EDM studies is to examine women's experiences beyond a United States context. As *Shejay*'s global roster of DJs confirms, women are pursuing DJing in EDM scenes worldwide. The recent increase in the number of women producing EDM introduces more opportunities for research that focuses on their music-making processes and their progress in various geographical and virtual locations. Additionally, women working behind the scenes at record labels, in clubs and in management positions are also important figures with much to contribute to this story. Further studies investigating gender issues in male-centric artistic and technology spaces other than music genres are also much needed.

In her discussion of contemporary music in the global economy, Geraldine Bloustien (2009) stresses the centrality of experiential activities and their relationship to new forms of subjectivity. To begin moving the discussion in this direction I have articulated the connections between the personal experiences and opinions of female DJ and producers and the range of practices that impact their creativity and EDM experiences. Analyses of DJ sets and tracks produced by women can further focus the conversation on corporeality and subjectivity and result in greater understanding of the relationship between gender and emotions and the tensions between the mind and the body.

This project demonstrates some of the ways in which the tables are indeed turning. EDM is extremely dynamic. The gender imbalances in EDM culture are slowly dissipating as the number of female DJs and producers continues to grow. New subgenres are continually invented and along with them new EDM scenes are created. While this can make it difficult to acquire subcultural capital and always be 'in the know', it also presents further openings and opportunities for EDM artists. At the same time, new technologies and social tools are empowering and enabling artists to not only move forward with their DJ and production passions in increasingly creative ways, but to also connect with others who share and support their actions. As EDM continues to metamorphize, the number of women engaging with it as DJs and producers will surely continue to grow. It is my hope that as the number of women pursuing these efforts multiplies, so will their recognition and power, in turn enabling them to move further beyond the dance floor.

Appendix

List of Interviewees

Ashley Adams
Audio Angel [Rashida Clendening]

Barbarella [Barbara Mayers]

Chaostica
Charlotte the Baroness [Charlotte Kaufman]

DJ Amber [Amber Nixon]
DJ Ara [Heather Reagan]
DJ Aura [Tina Nerpio]
DJ Blondie [Ilana Pearlman]
DJ Denise [Denise Rees]
DJ Icon [Connie Wong]
DJ KT [Katie Pollard]
DJ Leah
DJ Miche [Michelle Higley]

Forest Green [Melissa Green]

J-Fi [Jamie Finck]

Kate Simko

Lady Espina [Natalia Espina]
Layla Dudley

Linzee [Lynn Butta]
Liz Wheeler

Melissa [Melissa Burnell]
Melyss [Melissa Sautter]
Minx [Jennifer Witcher]

Polywog [Rebecca Corbett]

Queen Agnes B [Agnes Borysewicz]

Roxanne [Roxanne Mayoral]

Samira [Samira Vijghen]
Sappho [Megan Andricos]
SarahFAB [Sarah Pascoe]
Sarah LeWinter
Seraphim/DeLush [Sarah Randolph]
Shalimar Johnson

Tyler Stone

XJS [Annie Shaw]

References

Aaker, David A. (1991), *Managing Brand Equity: Capitalizing on the Value of a Brand Name*. New York: Maxwell Macmillan International.

Anderson, Tammy (2009), *Rave Culture: The Alteration and Decline of a Philadelphia Music Scene*. Philadelphia: Temple University Press.

Androutsopoulos, Jannis K. (2001), 'What Names Reveal About the Music Style: A Study of Naming Patterns in Popular Music', in E. Németh (ed.), *Pragmatics in 2000: Selected Papers from the 7th International Pragmatics Conference, Vol. 2*. Antwerp: International Pragmatics Association, pp. 16–29.

Anon (1916), 'The Feminine Wireless Amateur', *The Electrical Experimenter*, 16 October [online] Available at: <http://earlyradiohistory.us/1916fem.htm> (Accessed 9 March 2011).

———. (year unknown), 'Sistersf.com: Pushing the Envelope of Electronic Music in San Francisco', *Aboutus.org* [online] Available at: <http://aboutus.org/Sistersf.com> (Accessed 10 November 2010).

———. (2004), 'Beauty and the Beat', *Playboy Magazine*, April, pp. 72–77.

Arnold, David O. (ed.) (1973), *Subcultures*, Berkeley: The Glendessary Press.

Baker, Sarah (2008), 'From Snuggling and Snogging to Sampling and Scratching: Girls' Nonparticipation in Community-Based Music Activities', *Youth and Society* 39: 3, pp. 316–339.

Barrett, J. (2001), 'DJ Kimberly S.: Breaks the Barrier Between Gay Male and Lesbian Dance Music', *Advocate*, 14 August, p. 77.

Baym, Nancy K. (1999), *Tune In, Log On: Soaps, Fandom, and Online Community*. Thousand Oaks: Sage.

———. (2007), 'The New Shape of Online Community: The Example of Swedish Independent Music Fandom', *First Monday* 12: 8 [online] Available at: <http://firstmonday.org/htbin/cgiwrap/bin/ojs/index.php/fm/article/view/1978/1853> (Accessed 10 August 2010).

———. (2010), *Personal Connections in the Digital Age*. Cambridge: Polity.

Bayton, Mavis (1998), *Frock Rock: Women Performing Popular Music*. New York: Oxford University Press.

Bleyer, Jennifer (2004), 'Cut-and-Paste Revolution: Notes from the Girl Zine Explosion', in V. Labato and D. L. Martin (eds), *The Fire This Time: Young Activists and the New Feminism*. New York: Anchor Books, pp. 42–60.

Boyd, d (2008), 'Why Youth (Heart) Social Network Sites: The Role of Networked Publics in Teenage Social Life', in D. Buckingham (ed.), *Youth, Identity, and Digital Media*. Cambridge, MA: MIT Press, pp. 119–142.

Bradby, Barbara (1993), 'Sampling Sexuality: Gender, Technology and the Body in Dance Music', *Popular Music* 12, pp. 155–176.

Braithwaite, Ann (2004), 'Politics of/and Backlash', *Journal of International Women's Studies* 5: 5, pp. 18–33.

Brake, Michael (1985), *Comparative Youth Culture*. New York: Routledge.

Bredin, Marian (1991), 'Feminist Cultural Politics: Women in Community Radio in Canada', *Resources for Feminist Research* 20: 1–2, pp. 36–41.

Brewster, Bill and Broughton, Frank (2000), *Last Night a DJ Saved My Life: The History of the Disc Jockey*. New York: Grove Press.

British Broadcasting Corporation (2005), *Cornwall's DJ Name Finder Game* [online] Available at: <http://www.bbc.co.uk/cornwall/clubbing/quiz/quiz.shtml> (Accessed 10 July 2010).

Burbules, Nicholas C. and Rice, Suzanne (1991), 'Dialogue Across Difference: Continuing the Conversation', *Harvard Educational Review* 61, pp. 393–416.

Butler, Mark J. (2006), *Unlocking the Groove: Rhythm, Meter, and Musical Design in Electronic Dance Music*. Bloomington, IN: Indiana University Press.

Carlat, Louis. (1998), 'A Cleanser for the Mind: Marketing Radio Receivers for the American Home, 1922–1932', in R. Horowitz and A. Mohun (eds), *His and Hers: Gender, Consumption, and Technology*. Charlottesville: University Press of Virginia, pp. 115–138.

Carson, Mina, Lewis, Tisa and Shaw, Susan M. (2004), *Girls Rock! Fifty Years of Women Making Music*. Lexington: University Press of Kentucky.

Carter, Susan. (2004), 'A Mic of Her Own: Stations, Collectives, and Women's Access to Radio', *Journal of Radio Studies* 1: 2, pp. 169–183.

Christie, Alice A. (2005), 'How Middle School Boys and Girls View Today's Computer Culture', *Meridian* 8: 1 [online] Available at: <http://www.ncsu.edu/meridian/win2005/computer culture/index.html> (Accessed 18 January 2007).

Clarke, John (2007), 'Style', in S. Hall and T. Jefferson (eds), *Resistance Through Rituals*, second edn. London: Routledge, pp. 147–161.

Clawson, Mary Anne (1999), 'Masculinity and Skill Acquisition in the Adolescent Rock Band', *Popular Music* 18: 1, pp. 99–114.

Coates, Norma (1997), '(R)evolution Now? Rock and the Political Potential of Gender', in S. Whiteley (ed.), *Sexing the Groove: Popular Music and Gender*. New York: Routledge, pp. 50–64.

———. (1998), '"Can't We Just Talk About Music?": Rock and Gender on the Internet', in T. Swiss, J. Sloop and A. Herman (eds), *Mapping the Beat: Popular Music and Contemporary Theory*. Malden: Blackwell Publishers, pp. 77–99.

Cockburn, Cynthia (1985), *Machinery of Dominance: Women, Men, and Technical Know-How*. Dover: Pluto.

Cockburn, Cynthia and Ormrod, Susan (1993), *Gender and Technology in the Making*. Thousand Oaks: Sage.

Cohen, Sarah (1997), 'Men Making a Scene: Rock Music and the Production of Gender', in S. Whiteley (ed.), *Sexing the Groove: Popular Music and Gender*. New York: Routledge, pp. 17–36.

References

Cooper, Louise (2007), 'The Gender Factor: Teaching Composition in Music Technology Lessons to Boys and Girls in Year 9', in J. Finney and P. Burnard (eds), *Music Education with Digital Technology*. London: Continuum, pp. 30–40.

Cott, Nancy F. (1987), *The Grounding of Modern Feminism*. New Haven: Yale University Press.

Davis, Scott M. (2002), *Brand Asset Management: Driving Profitable Growth Through Your Brands*. San Francisco: Jossey-Bass.

Davis, Scott, Dunn, Michael and Aaker, David A. (2002), *Building the Brand-Driven Business: Operationalize Your Brand to Drive Profitable Growth*. San Francisco: Jossey-Bass.

Dicker, Rory and Piepmeier, Alison (2003), *Catching a Wave: Reclaiming Feminism for the 21st Century*. Boston: Northeastern.

Douglas, George H. (1987), *The Early Days of Radio Broadcasting*. Jefferson: McFarland.

Douglas, Susan (1995), *Where the Girls Are: Growing Up Female with the Mass Media*. New York: Three Rivers Press.

———. (2010), *Enlightened Sexism: The Seductive Message that Feminism's Work is Done*. New York: Times Books.

Driver, Susan (2007), *Queer Girls and Popular Culture: Reading, Resisting, and Creating Media*. New York: Peter Lang.

Ellison, Nicole, Lampe, Cliff, Steinfield, Charles, and Vitak, Jessica. (2010), 'With a Little Help from My Friends: Social Network Sites and Social Capital', in Z. Papacharissi (ed.), *A Networked Self: Identity, Community and Culture on Social Network Sites*. New York: Routledge, pp. 124–145.

Ellison, Nicole, Steinfield, Cliff and Lampe, Charles (2007), 'The Benefits of Facebook "Friends": Exploring the Relationship Between College Students' Use of Online Social Networks and Social Capital', *Journal of Computer-Mediated Communication* 12:3 [online] Available at: <http://onlinelibrary.wiley.com/doi/10.1111/j.1083-6101.2007.00367.x/full> (Accessed 12 January 2008).

Erdmann, Michael (2006), 'Plastikman Logo', weblog post, 12 June, <http://www.canadiandesignresource.ca/officialgallery/logo/plastikman-logo> (Accessed 18 September 2010).

Faludi, Susan (1991), *Backlash: The Undeclared War Against American Women*. New York: Doubleday.

Fikentscher, Kai (2000), *'You Better Work!' Underground Dance Music in New York City*. Hanover: University Press of New England.

Fiore, Catherine (1999), 'Awakening the Tech Bug in Girls', *Learning and Leading with Technology* 26, 10–17 [online] Available at: <http://www.iste.org/Content/NavigationMenu/Publications/LL/LLIssues/> (Accessed 14 November 2007).

Foucault, Michel (1980) (author), C. Gordon (ed.), *Power/Knowledge: Selected Interviews and Other Writings, 1972–1977*. New York: Vintage.

———. (1988), 'Technologies of the Self', in L. H. Martin, H. Gutman and P. H. Hutton (eds), *Technology of the Self: A Seminar with Michel Foucault*. Amherst, MA: University of Massachusetts Press, pp. 16–49.

Frith, Simon (1981), *Sound Effects*. New York: Pantheon.

———. (ed.) (2003), *Popular Music: Critical Concepts in Media and Cultural Studies*. New York: Routledge.

Garrison, Ednie K. (2000), 'US Feminism – Grrrl Style!: Youth (Sub)cultures and the Technologics of the Third Wave', *Feminist Studies* 26: 1, pp. 141–170.

Gilbert, Jeremy and Pearson, Ewan (1999), *Discographies: Dance, Music, Culture and the Politics of Sound*. New York: Routledge.

Gottlieb, Joanne and Wald, Gayle (1994), 'Smells Like Teen Spirit: Riot Grrrls, Revolution and Women in Independent Rock', in A. Ross and T. Rose (eds), *Microphone Fiends: Youth Music and Youth Culture*. New York: Routledge, pp. 250–274.

Gray, Ann (2002), *Research Practice for Cultural Studies: Ethnographic Methods and Lived Cultures*. Thousand Oaks: Sage.

Green, Eileen (2001), 'Technology, Leisure and Everyday Practices', in E. Green and A. Adams (eds), *Virtual Gender: Technology, Consumption and Identity Matters*. New York: Routledge, pp. 173–188.

Green, Lucy (1997), *Music, Gender, Education*. New York: Cambridge University Press.

———. (2005), 'Musical Meaning and Social Reproduction: A Case for Retrieving Autonomy', *Educational Philosophy and Theory* 37: 1, pp. 77–92.

Grossberg, Lawrence (1998), 'Re-Placing Popular Culture', in S. Redhead, D. Wynne and J. O'Connor (eds), *The Clubcultures Reader: Readings in Popular Cultural Studies*. Malden: Blackwell, pp. 199–219.

Guevara, Nancy (1996), 'Women Writin' Rappin' Breakin'', in W. E. Perkins (ed.), *Droppin' Science: Critical Essays on Rap Music and Hip Hop Culture*. Philadelphia: Temple University Press, pp. 49–62.

Hall, Stuart and Jefferson, Tony (1976), *Resistance Through Rituals: Youth Subcultures in Post-War Britain*. New York: HarperCollins.

Hall, Stuart and Whannel, Paddy (1965), *The Popular Arts*. London: Pantheon.

Harris, Anita (2004), *Future Girl: Young Women in the Twenty-First Century*. New York: Routledge.

Haslam, David (1998), 'DJ Culture', in S. Redhead, D. Wynne and J. O'Connor (eds), *The Clubcultures Reader: Readings in Popular Cultural Studies*. Malden: Blackwell, pp. 150–161.

Hebdige, Dick (1979), *Subculture: The Meaning of Style*. New York: Routledge.

Henry, Astrid (2004), *Not My Mother's Sister: Generational Conflict and Third-Wave Feminism*. Bloomington: Indiana University Press.

Hesmondhalgh, David (1998), 'The British Dance Music Industry: A Case Study of Independent Cultural Production', *The British Journal of Sociology* 49: 2, pp. 234–251.

Herman, Bill D. (2006), 'Scratching Out Authorship: Representations of the Electronic Music DJ at the Turn of the 21st Century', *Popular Communication* 4: 1, pp. 21–38.

Hodkinson, Paul (2002), *Goth: Identity, Style and Subculture*. Oxford: Berg.

Holt, Douglas B., Quelch, John A., and Taylor, E. L. (2004), 'How Global Brands Compete', *Harvard Business Review* 82: 9, pp. 68–75.

Hubbard, Ruth. (1983), 'Foreword', in J. Rothschild (ed.), *Macina Ex Dea: Feminist Perspectives on Technology*. New York: Pergamon, pp. vii–viii.

Hull, Geoffrey P. (2004), *The Recording Industry*. New York: Routledge.

Jenkins, Henry (2006), *Convergence Culture: Where Old and New Media Collide*. New York: New York University Press.

Kapferer, Jean-Noël (1997), *Strategic Brand Management: Creating and Sustaining Brand Equity Long Term*, second edn. London: Kogan Page.

Kearney, Mary C. (1997), 'The Missing Links: Riot Grrrl – Feminism – Lesbian Culture', in S. Whiteley (ed.), *Sexing the Groove: Popular Music and Gender*. New York: Routledge, pp. 207–229.

———. (2006), *Girls Make Media*. New York: Routledge.

Keightley, Keir (1996), '"Turn it Down!" She Shrieked: Gender, Domestic Space, and High Fidelity, 1948–59', *Popular Music* 15: 2, pp. 149–177.

Kenney, William H. (1999), *Recorded Music in American Life: The Phonograph and Popular Memory, 1890–1945*. New York: Oxford University Press.

Keyes, Cheryl (2002), *Rap Music and Street Consciousness*. Urbana and Chicago: University of Illinois Press.

Klein, N. (1997), *No Logo: Taking Aim at the Brand Bullies*. Picador, USA: New York.

Koerber, Amy (2001), 'Postmodernism, Resistance, and Cyberspace: Making Rhetorical Spaces for Feminist Mothers on the Web', *Women's Studies in Communication* 24: 2, pp. 218–240.

Kruse, Holly (1993), 'Subcultural Identity in Alternative Music', *Popular Music* 12: 1, pp. 33–41.

———. (2003), *Site and Sound: Understanding Independent Music Scenes*. New York: Peter Lang.

LeBlanc, Lauraine (1999), *Pretty in Punk: Girls' Gender Resistance in a Boys' Subculture*. New Brunswick: Rutgers University Press.

Leonard, Marion (1997), '"Rebel Girl, You are the Queen of my World": Feminism, "Subculture" and Grrrl Power', in S. Whiteley (ed.), *Sexing the Groove: Popular Music and Gender*. New York: Routledge, pp. 230–256.

———. (2007), *Gender in the Music Industry*. Burlington: Ashgate.

Martin, P. Y. (1990), 'Rethinking Feminist Organizations', *Gender & Society* 4: 2, pp. 182–206.

Martin, Daniel (1999), 'Power Play and Party Politics: The Significance of Raving', *Journal of Popular Culture* 32: 1, pp. 77–99.

Mazzarella, Sharon R. (2005), *Girl Wide Web: Girls, the Internet, and the Negotiation of Identity*. New York: Peter Lang.

McClary, Susan (1991), *Feminine Endings: Music, Gender, and Sexuality*. Minneapolis: University of Minnesota Press.

———. (2000), *Conventional Wisdom: The Content of Musical Form*. Berkeley, CA: University of California Press.

———. (2004), *Modal Subjectivities: Self-fashioning in the Italian Madrigal*. Berkeley, CA: University of California Press.

McCollum, B. (2001), 'The World Takes Notice of Electronic Music Event. Showcase Growing for Detroit Festival in May'. *Detroit Free Press* [online] 29 March. Available at: <http://www.freep.com/entertainment/index.htm> (Accessed 31 March 2001).

McLeod, Kembrew (2001), 'Genres, Subgenres, Sub-Subgenres and More: Musical and Social Differentiation Between Electronic/Dance Music Communities', *Journal of Popular Music* 13: 1, pp. 59–75.

———. (2002), 'Between Rock and a Hard Place: Gender and Rock Criticism', in S. Jones (ed.), *Pop Music and the Press*. Philadelphia: Temple University Press, pp. 93–113.

———. (2005), *Freedom of Expression: Overzealous Copyright Bozos and Other Enemies of Creativity*. New York: Doubleday.

McRobbie, Angela (1988), 'Peggy Sue Got Marketed', *Times Higher Education Supplement*, 3 June, p. 24.

———. (1994), *Postmodernism and Popular Culture*. New York: Routledge.

———. (2009), *The Aftermath of Feminism: Gender, Culture and Social Change*. Thousand Oaks: Sage.

McRobbie, Angela and Garber, Jennifer (1975/1997), 'Girls and Subcultures', in K. Gelder and S. Thornton (eds), *The Subcultures Reader*. New York: Routledge, pp. 112–120.

Meintjes, Louise (1993), *Sound of Africa! Making Music Zulu in a South African Studio*. Durham: Duke University Press.

Mitchell, Caroline (2000a), 'Sisters are Doing It … from Fem FM to Viva! A History of Contemporary Women's Radio Stations in the UK', in C. Mitchell (ed.), *Women and Radio: Airing Differences*. New York: Routledge, pp. 94–110.

———. (2000b), 'On Air/Off Air: Defining Women's Radio Space in European Women's Community Radio', in C. Mitchell (ed.), *Women and Radio: Airing Differences*. New York: Routledge, pp. 189–201.

Murphy, John M. (1987), *Branding: A Key Marketing Tool*. New York: McGraw-Hill.

Muggleton, David and Weinzierl, Rupert (2004), 'What is "Post-Subcultural Studies" Anyway?', in D. Muggleton and R. Weinzierl (eds), *The Post-Subcultures Reader*. New York: Berg, pp. 3–23.

Negus, Keith (1992), *Producing Pop: Culture and Conflict in the Popular Music Industry*. London: Edward Arnold.

———. (1998), 'Cultural Production and the Corporation: Musical Genres and the Strategic Management of Creativity in the US Recording Industry', *Media, Culture & Society* 20: 3, pp. 359–379.

———. (1999), *Music Genres and Corporate Cultures*. New York: Routledge.

North, Adrian S. and Noyes, Jan M. (2002), 'Gender Influences on Children's Computer Attitudes and Cognitions', *Computers in Human Behavior* 18: 2, pp. 135–150.

Oakes, Kaya (2009), *Slanted and Enchanted: The Evolution of Indie Culture*. New York: Holt Paperbacks.

Oldenziel, Ruth (1999), *Making Technology Masculine: Men, Women and Modern Machines in America 1870–1945*. Amsterdam: Amsterdam University Press.

Ormrod, Susan (1995), 'Feminist Sociology and Methodology: Leaky Black Boxes in Gender/ Technology Relations', in K. Grint and R. Gill (eds), *The Gender-Technology Relation: Contemporary Theory and Research*. London: Taylor and Francis, pp. 31–47.

Ott, Brian L. and Herman, Bill D. (2003), 'Mixed Messages: Resistance and Reappropriation in Rave Culture', *Western Journal of Communication* 67, pp. 249–270.

Owyang, Jeremiah (2008), *Social Network Stats: Facebook, MySpace, Reunion* [online] Available at: <http://www.web-strategist.com/blog/2008/01/09/social-network-stats-facebook-myspace-reunion-jan-2008/> (Accessed 11 June 2008).

Piano, Doreen (2004), 'Resisting Subjects: DIY Feminism and the Politics of Style in Subcultural Production', in D. Muggleton and R. Weinzierl (eds), *The Post-Subcultures Reader.* New York: Bergn, pp. 253–265.

Pini, Maria (2001), *Club Cultures and Female Subjectivity: The Move from Home to House.* Hampshire: Palgrave Macmillan.

Pomerantz, Shauna, Currie, Dawn H. and Kelly, Deirdre M. (2004), 'Sk8er Girls: Skateboarders, Girlhood and Feminism in Motion', *Women's Studies International Forum* 27, pp. 547–557.

Porcello, Thomas (1991), 'Speaking of Sound: Language and the Professionalization of Sound-Recording Engineers', *Social Studies of Science* 34: 5, pp. 733–758.

———. (2004), 'Afterword', in P. D. Greene and T. Porcello (eds), *Wired for Sound: Engineering and Technologies in Sonic Cultures.* Middletown: Wesleyan University Press, pp. 269–281.

Poschardt, U. (1998), *DJ Culture.* Translated from German by S. Whiteside. London: Quartet Books.

Pough, Gwendolyn (2004), *Check It While I Wreck It: Black Womanhood, Hip Hop Culture, and the Public Sphere.* Boston: Northeastern University Press.

Putnam, Robert (2000), *Bowling Alone: The Collapse and Revival of American Community.* New York: Simon and Schuster.

Raphael, Amy (1996), *Grrrls: Viva Rock Divas.* New York: St. Martin's Press.

Reddington, Helen (2003), '"Lady" Punks in Bands: A Subculturette?', in D. Muggleotn and S. Weinzierl (eds), *The Post Subcultures Reader.* New York: Berg, pp. 239–251.

———. (2007), *The Lost Women of Rock Music.* Hampshire: Ashgate.

Redhead, Steve, Wynne, Derek and O'Connor, Justin (eds) (1998), *The Clubcultures Reader: Readings in Popular Cultural Studies.* Malden: Blackwell

Reynolds, Simon (1998), 'Rave Culture: Living Dream or Living Death?', in S. Redhead, D. Wynne and J. O'Connor (eds), *The Clubcultures Reader: Readings in Popular Cultural Studies.* Malden: Blackwell, pp. 84–93.

———. (1999), *Generation Ecstasy: Into the World of Techno and Rave Culture.* New York: Routledge.

Reynolds, Simon and Press, Joy (1996), *The Sex Revolts: Gender, Rebellion, and Rock 'n' Roll.* Cambridge: Harvard University Press.

Rheingold, Howard (1994), *The Virtual Community: Homesteading on the Electronic Frontier.* New York: HarperPerennial.

Rodgers, Tara (2003), 'On the Process and Aesthetics of Sampling in Electronic Music Production', *Organized Sound* 8: 3, pp. 313–320.

Rodgers, T. (2010), *Pink Noises: Women on Electronic Music and Sound.* Durham: Duke University Press.

Roiphe, Katie (1993), *The Morning After: Sex, Fear, and Feminism on Campus.* Boston: Little, Brown and Company.

Rose, Tricia (1994), *Black Noise: Rap Music and Black Culture in Contemporary America.* Hanover: Weslyan University Press.

Rozin, Randall S. and Magnusson, Liz (2003), 'Processes and Methods for Creating a Global Business-to-Business Brand', *Journal of Brand Management* 10: 3, pp. 185–207.

Sandstrom, Boden (2000), 'Women Mix Engineers and the Power of Sound', in P. Moisala and B. Diamond (eds), *Music and Gender*. Chicago: University of Illinois Press, pp. 289–305.

Scott, Derek, B. (2009), 'Introduction', in D. B. Scott (ed.), *Ashgate Research Companion to Popular Musicology*. Burlington, VT: Ashgate, pp. 1–21.

Sicko, Dan (1999), *Techno Rebels: A Unique Narrative of the Evolution and Revolution of Techno Music*. New York: Billboard Books.

Siegler, D. (2002), 'Sounding Off', *Pinknoises.com: The One-Stop Web Resource on Women and Electronic Music* [online] Available at: <http://www.pinknoises.com/soundoff.shtml> (Accessed 20 September 2003).

Silcott, Mireille (1999), *Rave America: New School Dancescapes*. Toronto: ECW Press.

Sloboda, John (2001), 'Emotion, Functionality and the Everyday Experience of Music: Where Does Music Education Fit?', *Music Education Research* 3: 2, pp. 243–253.

Snyder-Hall, R. Claire (2010), 'Third-Wave Feminism and the Defense of "Choice"', *Symposium* 8: 1, pp. 255–261.

Soapboxgirls (2000), 'The Technology Issue: DJ Dazy', weblog post, November [online] Available: <http://www.djdazy.com/interviewshtml> (Accessed 14 June 2010).

Spencer, Amy (2008), *DIY: The Rise of Lo-Fi Culture*. London: Marion Boyars Publishers.

Stahl, Geoff (2004), 'Tastefully Renovating Subcultural Theory: Making Space for a New Model', in D. Muggleton and R. Weinzierl (eds), *The Post-Subcultures Reader*. New York: Berg, pp. 27–40.

Stanton Magnetics (2007) [online] Available at: <http://www.stantonmagnetics.com/v2/index.asp> (Accessed 6 June).

Steiner, Linda (2005), 'The Feminist Cable Collective as Public Sphere Activity', *Journalism* 6: 3, pp. 313–334.

Sterling, S. (1999), '10 Reasons to Love DJ Rap', *Velocity: Accelerated Culture* 4: 2, p. 48.

Straw, Will (1997), 'Sizing Up Record Collections: Gender and Connoisseurship in Rock Music Culture', in S. Whiteley (ed.), *Sexing the Groove: Popular Music and Gender*. New York: Routledge, pp. 3–16.

Susan, Driver (2007), *Queer Girls and Popular Culture*. New York: Peter Lang.

Taft, Jessica K. (2004), 'Girl Power Politics: Pop-Culture Barriers and Organizational Resistance', in A. Harris (ed.), *All About the Girl: Culture, Power, and Identity*. New York: Routledge, pp. 69–78.

Taylor, Timothy D. (2001), *Strange Sounds: Music, Technology and Culture*. New York: Routledge.

Technics (2007) [online] Available at: <http://www.panasonic-europe.com/technics> (Accessed 6 June).

Technics1200s Service Center [online] Available at: <http://www.1200s.com> (Accessed 6 June).

Terrett, Piper (2003), *Bedroom DJ: A Beginner's Guide*. London: Omnibus Press.

Théberge, Paul (1991), 'Musicians' Magazines in the 1980s: The Creation of a Community and a Consumer Market', *Cultural Studies* 5: 3, pp. 270–293.

Théberge, Paul (1997), *Any Sound You Can Image: Making Music/Consuming Technology*. Hanover: Wesleyan University Press.

Thinkbox New Media Collective (2004) [online] Available at: <http://www.thinkbox.ca> (Accessed 16 September).

Thompson, Haven (2009), 'Invasion of the Dilettante DJs', *W Magazine*, December, pp. 106–108.

Thornton, Sarah (1996), *Club Cultures: Music, Media, and Subcultural Capital*. Hanover: Wesleyan University Press.

——. (1997), 'Introduction', in K. Gelder and S. thornton (eds), *The Subcultures Reader*. New York: Routledge, pp. 1–7.

Travers, Ann (2003), 'Parallel Subaltern Feminist Counterpublics in Cyberspace', *Sociological Perspectives* 46: 2, pp. 223–237.

Tropical-house.com (2010) [online] Available at: <http://tropical-house.com/residents/djdazy.htm> (Accessed 15 October).

van Zoonen, Elizabeth A. (1992), 'The Women's Movement and the Media: Constructing a Public Identity', *European Journal of Communication* 7: 4, pp. 453–476.

Velocity: Accelerated Culture (1999), 'The Girly Issue', 4.2.

Vignoli, Fabio (2004), 'Digital Music Interaction Concepts: A User Study', in *Proceedings of International Symposium for Music Information Retrieval, ISMIR*.

Wagner, D. (2011), 'Bay Area DJs Shatter Sexist Preconceptions', *San Francisco Chronicle and SFGate.com*. 10 April.

Wald, Gayle (1998), 'Just a Girl? Rock Music, Feminism, and the Cultural Construction of Female Youth', *Signs: Journal of Women in Culture and Society* 23: 3, pp. 585–610.

Walser, Robert (2008), 'Uninvited: Gender, Schizophrenia, and Alanis Morissette', in S. Baur, R. Knapp and J. Warwick (ed.), *Musicological Identities: Essays in Honor of Susan McClary*. Burlington, VT: Ashgate, pp. 235–242.

Wajcman, Judy (1991), *Feminism Confronts Technology*. University Park: Penn State University Press.

——. (2004), *Techno Feminism*. Malden: Polity Press.

Walker, Rebecca (2001), 'Becoming the Third Wave', in B. Ryan (ed.), *Identity Politics in the Women's Movement*. New York: New York University Press, pp. 78–80.

Walther, Joseph B. (1992), 'Interpersonal Effects in Computer-Mediated Interaction: A Relational Perspective', *Communication Research* 19, pp. 52–90.

Wehner, Cyclone (2000), 'The Fourth Wave: Techno and Gender' [online] Available at: <http://www.tribemagazine.com/board/techno-room/21269-techno-gender.html>(Accessed 1 November from http://www.undergroundcommittee.com/4thwave.htm).

Wellman, Barry (2001), 'Physical Place and Cyberspace: The Rise of Personalized Networking', *International Journal of Urban and Regional Research* 25: 2, 227–252.

Whiteley, Sheila (1998), 'Repressive Representations: Patriarchy and Femininities in Rock Music of the Counterculture', in T. Swiss, J. Sloop, and A. Herman (eds), *Mapping the Beat: Popular Music and Contemporary Theory*. Malden: Blackwell, pp. 153–170.

——. (2000), *Women and Popular Music: Sexuality, Identity and Subjectivity*. New York: Routledge.

Wilson, Fiona (2003), 'Can Compute, Won't Compute: Women's Participation in the Culture of Computing', *New Technology, Work and Employment* 18: 2, pp. 127–142.

Willis, Paul (1991), 'Notes on Method', in S. Hall, D. Hobson, A. Lowe and P. Willis (eds), *Culture, Media, Language: Working Papers in Cultural Studies, 1972–1979*. London: Routledge, pp. 153–170.

Willis, Paul and Trondman, Mats (2002), 'Manifesto for Ethnography', *Cultural Studies < = >Critical Methodologies* 2: 3, pp. 394–402.

Women's Airwaves Survey (2002), 'Women's Airwaves Collective', in C. Mitchell (ed), *Women and Radio: Airing Differences*. London: Routledge, pp. 84–93.

Wright, April (2002), 'Technology as an Enabler of Global Branding in Retail Financial Services', *Journal of International Marketing* 10: 2, pp. 83–98.

XL Music: Promotions and Bookings (2010), 'DJ Portia Surreal' [online] Available at: <http://www.xlmusic.gr/modern/xlmusic_djs/international_djs_and_artists/34/dj_portia_surreal.scratch#more-34> (Accessed 14 June).

Yancey Martin, P. (1990), 'Rethinking Feminist Organizations', *Gender & Society* 4, pp. 182–206.

Websites

Brands of the World [online], 2010. Available at: <http:www.brandsoftheworld.com> (Accessed 18 September 2010).

Crobar Nightclub [online] Available at: <http://www.crobar.com> (Accessed 6 June 2006).

Dj.com [online], 2010. Available at: <http://www.dj.com> (Accessed 29 June).

Djicon.com [online], 2010. Available at: <http://www.djicon.com> (Accessed 14 June).

DJrap.com [online], 2010. Available at: <http://www.djrap.com> (Accessed 14 June).

Portiasurreal.com [online], 2010. Available at: <http://www.portiasurreal.com> (Accessed 14 June).

Shejay.com [online], 2001/2010. Available at: <http://www.shejay.com> (Accessed 15 November 2001; 13 October 2010).

Sisterdjs.com [online], 2003. (Accessed 10 September).

SisterNYC.com [online], 2006. (Accessed 27 July).

SisterPDX.com [online], 2006. (Accessed 27 July).

SisterSF.com [online], 2006. (Accessed 1 October).

Stanton Magnetics [online], 2007. Available at: <http://www.stantonmagnetics.com/v2/index.asp> (Accessed 6 June).

Technics [online], 2007. Available at: <http://www.panasonic-europe.com/technics> (Accessed 6 June).

Technics1200s Service Center [online], 2007. Available at: <http://www.1200s.com> (Accessed 6 June).

Thinkbox New Media Collective [online], 2004. Available at: <http://www.thinkbox.ca> (Accessed 16 September).

Tropical-house.com [online], 2010. Available at: <http://tropical-house.com/residents/djdazy.htm> (Accessed 15 October).

Index

V

Velo *see* Dudley, Layla
Verein Stadtimpuls Wien (Vienna City
    Impulse Association)   136
Viera-Newton, Harley   43–4
Vijghen, Samira (Samira)   82–3, 99, 107,
    108, 110–11, 125–6
Viva! radio station   101 *see also* radio

W

The Wade Robson Project MTV series   48
Warp label   120 *see also* record labels
websites   82–4, 144 *see also* Beatport.com,
    Internet, networking, Sistersf.com
white labels   30 *see also* record labels
Winter (Winter Clark)   111
Witcher, Jennifer (DJ Minx)   4, 27, 28, 127
Women on Wax   127 *see also* record labels

WOMN radio station   101 *see also* radio
Womyn's Music movement   93, 94, 95, 96
Wong, Connie (DJ Icon)   47–50
Wong, Jennifer   111
WWMN-AM radio station   101 *see also*
    radio

X

XJS (Annie Shaw)   75–6, 82, 98, 99–100,
    102–3, 106, 107, 108, 110, 123
XLR8R   6, 11, 129 *see also* magazines

Y

'Your Sister's House' event   97–8

Z

zines   84–5 *see also* e-zines, magazines
Zulu music   122–3